Ishmail Kamara published earlier

SMILE (Hafan Books 2018)
Landschap van mijn Ziel (WGBU 2021)

HUNDRED GOLDEN HORSES

A JOURNEY TO THE PROMISSED LAND

ISHMAIL KAMARA

WGBU
Rijswijk

ISBN 978-9-0834-2883-3

NUR 302

Dedicated to the travellers

Inhoud

Boyhood

The sky was dark grey with flashes of lightning which ignited some heavy thunder strikes cracking on the earth. As soon as we had started to prepare for the mystery hanging ahead of us, the sea breeze manifested into a violent storm and it began to drizzle.

The sails swayed in odd directions as the storm forced its way indiscriminately across every space between the gigantic white cotton cloths. Waves roared and banged as they hit the wooden sailing ship. The clinking sound of falling plates and spoons from the cabins below the deck rang a warning bell that something catastrophic was hanging on the horizon. The situation on-board became intense and I was terrified the wriggling boat was going to capsize at any moment.

Rainwater poured down from the heavenly sky, slapping us hard on the head like hailstones hitting an unsealed metal roof. The three of us on-board did our best to keep the sails steady and facing the right direction. The mist at sea was so thick that, from where I stood, I could barely see what was happening ahead of the boat.

After a while the storm ceased, but showers of blessings continued pouring down on the surface of the sea. The boat was starting to capsize and had already leaned low to one side.

"Land, there is land!" cried one of the men on-board , pointing with his index finger.

I turned around and glanced in the direction he had pointed. There was indeed land. It was flat, as flat as sea level, with hills that evoked an image of a sleeping lion manifested against the background of the beach.

My ears could barely handle the whimpering and barking of two furious wolves standing vigilantly close to a pretty but pale-looking woman dressed in a long white wedding dress. Her hair was charcoal black, thick and perfectly trimmed, and it fell behind her back with the sea breeze. The complexion of her bared feet standing steadfastly on the glittering sand matched the colour of her heart-shaped face, pale like snowflakes in the winter, and dry like fallen autumn leaves.

The figure on land stood motionless like a statue of the fisherman's wife who stood for years along the banks of the coast, longing for her love to return from the sea. Onboard, we searched desperately for a convenient dock, though our search was distracted by our unbreakable gaze at the woman on the shore. We were disturbed by the scene on the beach, which was obvious from the expression on our faces.

Suddenly, I realised the woman was my mother and I felt a surge of pity at her sorrowful look. After being arrested by such emotions my intuition told me that she was in danger, her flesh and blood standing motionless between two wild animals. I forgot about the troubles we had encountered with the rain and storm moments earlier and my soul caught an urge which commanded me to jump down to the shore and save my mother's life.

"Mama!" I shouted, with the most empathetic voice I had

ever spoken with.

The echo of my voice triggered a movement, and the woman began to fade away into the mist in the forest along the beach. Before I could jump to the shore to do something, she melted like salt dissolving into water, slowly, and continued fading away until she had become invisible.

I opened my eyes and glanced at my electronic clock. July the seventh, six-thirty in the morning.

I lifted my head up slightly and looked around me, like a sleeping cat suddenly awakening from its midnight sleep. With relief, I sighed and laid my cheek back on my pillow and relaxed again inside my sleeping bag.

I was soothed by my realisation that everything that had happened had just been a dream.

When humankind fall deeply into their slumber, their imagination takes them to places they have never been before.

With the combination of memories of their past and fantasies of their future, humankind will see pictures, visual illusions, images and other movements known as dreams.

And, behold, every dream has its own interpretation.

My name is Eba Yoko. I was born in a village called Pete Fu, a small village comprising twenty huts all built of red loam and roofed with bamboo thatch. Its tiny roads were unpaved, and most of its surroundings were natural and inhabited by a thick green rainforest. Our village was always alive as the sounds of singing birds ruled the day and that of stridulating crickets ruled the night.

The land was laid flat and swampy right at the foot of the Alligator River.

I didn't know exactly how old I was when I first calculated my age, but my father once told me that my mother gave birth to me during the dry season at the end of the brutal civil war which took the lives of thousands of innocent souls in my country.

"It is seven years since your mother passed away," my father told me one evening at the farm while I was busy scraping sheep manure, cleaning the shed.

On that day I decided I must be about seven, and I have counted my age every year since then.

In my village it is not unusual for people not to know their date of birth or how old they are. People are reminded of their birth date through past events such as the death of prominent men or the burning of farmlands.

Talking about age reminds me about a story during the war in my country.

The story is about a father who claimed that his son was older than him in order to save his own life. A hostile armed group stopped and questioned both the father and son about who was the eldest.

"Actually, I am his biological father, but he is really old. He might be even older than me," the father declared.

"Good Lord. How could your own son be older than you?" asked the rebel commandant.

The father couldn't respond to the question. He appeared to be panicking, and he started trembling. The rebel soldiers looked at each other and exploded with laughter as they set both father and son free.

"You are free to go, I never want you in my sight again!" said the rebel commandant. Before the commander could finish addressing them both father and son took off on their

feet. They ran as fast as young fawns escaping their predator, the father in the lead and son chasing behind.

The rebels were notorious for their acts of cruelty to ordinary civilians, though so was the army on the other hand.
During the war, it was a big challenge for people like
pregnant women, young girls, politicians or families to bail
themselves out. Especially when they fell into an ambush of
armed men.
The atrocities committed on innocent civilians by armed
forces were tangible. You can see shreds of evidence through
the scars left behind on the bodies and mind of their victims
all over the country, even in present times.

I was the only child who survived inside in my mother's
womb after she suffered five miscarriages. All five took place
during early pregnancy.
People referred to me as the mystery child who survived
for ten months inside my mother's womb before I was delivered to this mysterious world.
My father made it clear to me that those ten months were
the most difficult times of my mother's life.
My mother gave birth successfully to a healthy baby boy
which brought her and my father absolute happiness and
stability in their married life after several years of unhappi-
ness and misfortune.

Born at the doorstep of destitution, my father, Mamoudo
Yoko, was a hard- working rice farmer and a genuine palm
wine tapper, who in his early twenties had traditionally got
married to my mother, Bomporo Thullah.

Bomporo was a trustworthy farm-watch and passionate about growing organic vegetables. Their shared passion for farming made them a unique couple.

Their friendship was no coincidence as they had a lot in common.

Other women in our village used to tell me that my mother was the most adorable girl during her youth. One afternoon, along the main road, I crossed paths with a woman who used to be friends with my mother, and she told me,

"When your poor father fell in love with young Bomporo, he worshipped her from head to toe."

According to stories, my mother's bewitching looks captured the attention of men and put them under her spell. The queue of men was long as both young and old men lined up hoping to marry my mother.

My father was lucky, like a daylight robber escaping with his treasure. He was the prize winner, chosen over the rest by my mother. That cost him a fortune of two cows and cash, which he duly paid to his father-in-law in exchange for his bride.

My father's endless love for my mother was a fact that I can testify. Since I had become sensible enough to see things my own way, I had never seen my father with another woman. After my mother's death, he decided not to get married to another woman in this life. Sometimes I wonder whether her death strengthened their bond even more than it was when she was alive. I wonder if it was invisible but true that my mother's spirit was still with him, especially when he was alone.

Sometimes I heard my father murmuring to himself, alone inside my mother's old farm hut, and calling out her name.

He sounded like a spiritualist speaking in tongues but in a low tone.

During my boyhood, I used to wake up as early as the muezzin made his first call for the early morning prayers. I took the responsibility of waking my clan members up every morning for our traditional bird shooting and other early morning activities.

My self-made rubber sling, in which I used stones as bullets to shoot birds, was a treasure. My sling and I slept side by side as I had to protect it from potential intruders and, you never know, you might be sleeping under the same roof as the intruder.

After bird shooting, we went to pick ripe mangoes in the forbidden forest.

We were terrified of the forest but during the hard times of the rainy season we had no other choice but to enter that forbidden forest, break those forbidden rules and pick those forbidden ripe fruits people call mangoes.

In those days, we often had to go to bed without a proper meal as the rice reserves in most households had already been emptied by hands made by God.

I was the best mango picker in the group because I used a special tool made for me by my father. A long bamboo stick with a thin convex-shaped metal hook on the edge at the top of the cane stick. The convex metal and the two-and-a-half metre cane stick gave me the advantage of bringing down dozens of mangoes in one brush. That tool was called 'Go to Hell'.

My childhood friends called me by a nickname, 'man can

go', which means 'mango'.

Along the Alligator River, we used to climb the tall coconut trees and throw down coconut fruit we called 'jelly'. The collectors under the tree had to mind their heads. Coconuts can be harder than rocks. We had to work hard to peel the first layer of the young fruits as they are solidly attached to the underlayer, like a young ape holding on to its mother's stomach during a jump.

Jellies are the young coconuts, which still look very green but are filled with plenty of sweet and juicy coconut water.

We drank in abundance to quench our thirst and fill our bellies, but although it helped us during the day, there was not enough to go around for us to sleep well.

During the rainy season, the Alligator River flowed and provided an abundance of water, fish and crabs which led us to the activity of hook and bait fishing. I usually cooked the catch of the day for my father's evening meal.

As a boy, I played the role of a mother in my father's life despite our tradition that it is a woman who should play that role and take care of the cooking and domestic work in the house.

No one came to the aid of my father during that difficult period of time. According to our tradition, he was supposed to marry my mother's sister, who was willing to after my mother's death. My father's reluctance to remarry made life difficult for us. Because of our day to day struggle, our family bond was strong in a unique way that was beyond the comprehension of many of the native folk.

I grew up without an image of my mother in my mind. I never saw her preparing dinner for me, as mothers do for their children.

According to rumours, my mother went missing during a rebel attack in our village and since then nothing has been heard of her, though her body has never been found.

Some people believed that she was taken as a hostage by the rebels, while others believed she drowned in the river while she was trying to escape with me. I was still a baby when I was found, weeping and wailing, along the river bank during the aftermath of the attack. Several years after the end of a long conflict in our land, my mother was declared dead, but was never forgotten. My father tirelessly mourned the death of his late wife, and every year he invited friends and families from both his and my mother's side. They offered a sacrifice by slaughtering a white sheep and later they cooked the meat with vegetables into soup with rice. At the end of the ceremony everyone would eat and drink and say prayers for my late mother, which was the only thing we could do for her.

My father always made a promise to my mother's soul during the mourning ceremony. He promised that he would never marry another woman.

"I know you are there waiting for me Bomporo," my father would say encouragingly to himself.

The year I became ten years old, a man who I had never seen before showed up at my mother's annual memorial ceremony. He was dressed appropriately for the sombre occasion, in a decent dark tan suit with a white shirt underneath. I learned later that the man in the dark tan suit was one of my father's half-brothers, which meant he was my uncle in the first bloodline. During the ceremony, I observed that he was highly respected by the other family members. I later heard them discussing local politics. Their discussion revealed that he was highly informed, educated and active in politics. He was particularly vocal about political and economic issues, such as the price of a bag of rice or a gallon of fuel in urban cities. He seemed more interested in talking about politics than the main event, which was my mother's commemoration day.

At the end of the ceremony everyone left, except my uncle who had to spend the night at our house.

I became curious when he raised the subject of taking me with him. It sounded to me as if taking me with him was his main goal and the primary reason for him coming to our village. It was clear that he wanted to adopt me and take me to his house in a bigger town called Looking Town where he lived with his wife and children.

The expression on my father's face became bitter when my uncle made the request, though it appeared to be an agreement they had made earlier. An agreement which my father, an honest man, had no choice but to honour.

I heard my uncle say to my father, "The boy is now grown up enough to go to school. I will take him with me and make sure he has a better future."

It was his point about my schooling which finally convinced my father to let me go.

At that moment, I was engulfed by sadness. I was a ten-year-old boy, the only child of my father, whose world was full of dreams and ambitions. I was determined to work hard and make a difference in our home by the time I would become a man.

Inside his bedroom my father called me for a little advice. "Eba," he said, "you are a boy who is about to become a man. Go with your uncle and listen to whatever he says to you. Don't think of coming back to me if you do not obey his command. I believe in you. Go! You have my blessing." He shed a tear, as did I.

It was dark at my uncle's house as we arrived late at night. Everyone in the house was already asleep.

"Agnes!" my uncle called to his wife in a booming voice while simultaneously knocking loudly on the front door.

"Yes, I am on my way," she answered worriedly. The door was opened from inside.

"Why are you so late?" she asked.

"The minibus broke down twice on the way, and there was no other option but to wait there until it was fixed, which took half of the day."

It was true that the only bus in our surrounding area which served as public transport had indeed broken down twice on the way, and that situation had presented my uncle with an opportunity which he made good use of by drinking a spontaneous gallon of palm wine at each break down point. He walked on his toes by the time we arrived at his house and smelled strongly of alcohol.

"This is Eba, my son," he introduced me confidently, as if I were his biological child. "Eba will stay with us here in the house. He can play together with his brothers." The strong odour of alcohol which evaporated from his breath permeated the whole living room as he spoke. "He is a clever boy just like me," he said, "he will start going to school soon and make new friends."

"Welcome my son," Aunty Agnes responded in a tired voice. I could tell she was longing to return back to bed and cuddle her pillow. She picked up a light bed cover and a cushion from the couch and threw them to me.

"Take these," she muttered, "you can go inside the boy's room and sleep next to your brothers."

As I entered the room, I immediately recognised the smell of week-old urine and bed bugs. On the bed, two boys were soundly asleep in odd positions which left no space for me to fit in. I wondered whether they knew anything about me, the new family member who was about to join them. I spread the cotton bed cover on the floor next to the bed and quietly lowered my body down on to the ground, but I didn't fall asleep. I started missing my father and my friends from our troublesome group 'Home Clan' which was formed by me and two of my friends, Sembu and Yakuba. We were the youngest boy clan in our village, and the most notorious. We were known for the funny little things we did. Even though we were bullied many times by members of the 'Ojeh Clan', who were older than us, we stood strong in defiance of joining their sacred society.

When I opened my eyes, it was daylight. The two boys were already up and preparing to go to school. The room smelled of Vaseline mixed with burned palm oil. It was a smell I was familiar with as I used the same ointment after having a bath. The boys, after putting on their blue shirts and khaki shorts, left me laying on the floor without exchanging a word.

My uncle was a bogus and a rascal. He was the sort of man who would always boast of his ability and hard work.

He frequently talked about the suffering he had endured to build the dazzling yellow-painted house which he called his shrine. He had managed to escape the line of poverty that he and his brothers were born into, which he described as the tomb of indigence. During his early childhood, he was taken by a religious priest to Looking Town. My father told me the story about a priest who came to our village to help poor people with education and serious health challenges. After a few years of service in his mission, the priest left our village. He adopted my uncle and took him with him to Looking Town where he had the opportunity to go to school and later graduated with a bachelor's degree in theology. My uncle later changed his religious course and became a politician instead of a priest. It was a move which was, according to rumours from other family members, disappointing to the priest who had invested a lot in him and consequently had higher expectations that he would serve the purpose of God.

My uncle, Sanday Yoko, was well thought of among his friends who nicknamed him 'The Commoner'. That name was also his political charm. He used it wisely and successfully negotiated his way to the top class.

They have a phrase in our local language which means that something must happen by hook or crook. Uncle Sanday climbed the ladder and achieved his goal of becoming a politician, albeit a selfish one.

Throughout the Continent of the Lions, it was commonplace for people to get rich as soon they became involved in politics, or held any position in public office. Being corrupt became the normal practice, in the way officials ask for 'cold water' in return for their services, of every ordinary man in a government department. From police officers to school teachers. From permanent secretaries to first ministers. They became a united bunch of cankerworms, uncaring and feasting on the guts of the hungry masses.

My uncle always referred to my father as a lazy sleeping bear who didn't have any plans. He would shout loudly, like a mad person, while he drank his palm wine.

"The pot of the lazy man is always empty!" he would say to humiliate our poorer neighbours with his provocative expressions. Every day, I was the one who had to cater for his fresh tapped palm wine before the addicted drinkers rushed to the palm wine bar. He also enjoyed telling me how he was busy looking for a woman for my father to marry, which he believed could help wake my father up from his long-wasted slumbered life. He would say those reckless words at moments when his hairy, naked stomach had risen to its maximum point, probably due to the yeast that was used to ferment the commercialised palm wine he consumed every day. The question about my father's remarriage was an important one. In our tradition, a man without a wife is a man without values. Such men cannot be trusted to hold any position, even at the lowest levels of community leadership, or to speak in public meetings. Unfortunately, my father happened to fall neatly into such a stereotype, although one thing which made me proud was that my father drank his self-tapped palm wine, unpolluted and direct from God to man.

After a year, I experienced the next disappointment in my life when my uncle failed to send me to school as he had promised the previous year. That year was the decider of the educational part of my life. I grew up illiterate and it was a title which became a tumour in my life. I never forgot the promise my uncle had repeatedly made to me. "Eba, I will send you to school as soon as the next school semester commences." A promise he made, but which never came to pass, serving only to suspend me in the air as the years went by.

I never had the opportunity to set my foot on the doorstep of a classroom, and instead grew up to become an ordinary servant. I was the one who did all the dirty jobs in the house and washed the clothes, did the dishes, went to the market to buy groceries, and so the list goes on.

I was laughed at by other boys in our neighbourhood.

"When will you to be sent to school, old boy?" they shouted, laughing at me loudly as they made their way to school. Sometimes I threw stones at them like a mad person to scare them away, while hot tears flooded my face.

I had only one loyal friend, Alimamy.

Alimamy's mother had a small restaurant along the road main towards the town centre. Sometimes I helped her to pound cassava leaves, and she made life better for me by providing me with an extra plate of rice every working day.

That arrangement infuriated my uncle's wife, Agnes. She was a short and chubby woman who spoke with a sharp, authoritative voice. She was a figure people referred to in our local language as the 'Sowei' to my uncle, meaning that she was his medicine. Uncle Sanday, though highly regarded as a very important figure in the community, only listened to, believed or did what his wife decided. Aunty Agnes, as I was obliged to call her, accused me of bringing an atrocious reputation to the family by helping an ordinary food seller with 'cheap labour' as she referred to it, making out I had done something terrible like a man who has committed treason.

"This is a complete disgrace to our family, especially in the eyes of our neighbours," she said with fury and in response to her complaints I would be punished by my uncle. He whipped me, twelve strokes across my bared back with a dry cane stick, and if I cried out loud he would start all over again.

When I finally resigned myself to the fact that I had been deprived of my right to go to school, I tried to become smarter by joining my cousins whenever they were on a study group or did their homework at night. My uncle's children were well catered for by their parents in terms of education. The two boys, Mo and Sol, spoiled by their mother in the name of love, attended the Saint Angelico high school for boys, a private school where they both acquired a high-quality education. The girl, Gina, attended the private school for girls which offered boarding facilities, albeit only for children with surnames of families who had political influence or were connected to colonial masters. Gina used to come home during the school holidays. I was jealous of my cousins, and I blamed my father for not sending me to school and for warning me not to return to him even if things went wrong at my uncle's, but Gina was sympathetic and kind to me and I sensed that she thought it was unfair that her father, an influential man, didn't send me to school even though he could easily afford to do so.

"You are very smart Eba, you learn quickly," Gina would say to me whenever she gave me lessons on reading or letter writing. I was also good at spelling and sometimes even beat boys who were already in school during spelling challenges.

After the civil war was over the military regime continued recruiting the young, at the age of adolescence, into the
army against their will.

A year after a peace treaty had been signed by the various
fractions who took part in the civil war, the regime started
a new war due to a border dispute with our neighbouring
country. During the first civil war, the armed forces from
our neighbouring country, Nane, had deployed their sixth-
armed battalion. It was a deal made by the regime to help
them win the war against the rebels. Since then, the sixth-
armed battalion was deployed at the strategic border town
of Kennen which was known as the gold-rich area. Kennen
also had a sea-port along the river that formed the border
between the two countries. The border dispute began when
the sixth-battalion of the Nane armed forces refused to
leave the gold-rich town when they were asked to do so by
the regime. Instead they claimed that the town of Kennen
legitimately belonged to our country Yougosoba, and they
claimed the area was part of their Nane sovereignty. A few
months later, the border dispute became intense when the
foreign Nane troops began compelling citizens of Yougosoba
to pay taxes to the government of a neighbouring country.

Local fisherman were deprived of fishing in the river by
the foreign soldiers who were busy with the activity of gold
and diamond mining in the area.

The leader of the regime in our country, General M'banga,
then declared a new war on the neighbouring Republic of
Nane, who then became defiant when it came to the issue of
leaving the gold-rich Kennen.

Going back to war within a year of a peace treaty being signed, a treaty which had ended a long struggle and a brutal war, was a prospect that many people opposed. Whilst the majority agreed that the land belonged to our side, the big question on everyone's lips was whether it would be wiser to give it some time and to settle the matter around a table rather than using guns and going to war with our neighbours. The new tactics of the regime at the time were considered, by the majority of citizens, to be senseless.

The main opposition at the time was a small minority who believed the new move was a ploy by General M'banga to delay a democratic election, as the regime were under international pressure to hold elections as part of the peace deal.

General M'banga, refused to hold elections due to his firmly held belief which was that, in his own words, "Our country is still at war."

The general then passed a decree which said that each and every uneducated youth must join the army. Those who refused would face serious consequences and feel the full force of the law, being locked up behind bars for a long time as political prisoners.

One evening my uncle came home, half-drunk and holding a piece of paper with a typed note. In front of his wife and children he called, "Eba, come here!" as the smell of palm wine poured out through his sweat I went close to him with curiosity.

"Yes sir," I reported, as always.

"This is a form from the army that you are going to sign," he said, "you are going to join the army where you will become a real man." Everyone laughed as I frowned. I was about sixteen years old.

"I don't want to join the army!" I replied through my tears, while Sol, who was going to the university, laughed provocatively. I wanted to strike him on the nose, but I realised that would be the most stupid thing I could do.

My memories brought me to a state wherein sometimes I had to swim into my father's tears. I saw him when he wept so hard as he watched his only child step into the small wooden canoe boat at the river bank on the day I left my village. I wondered whether my father and I would ever see each other again, and why my father shed those tears as I was leaving as it was his decision to hand me over to his half-brother. Now I am growing up, and gradually becoming a man, I am beginning to understand why a real man has to cry. I am still swimming into the tears of my father whenever I imagine the agony and pain he had endured in losing the woman he loved. I believe that the tears on my father's cheeks will form a river running down to the heavens, where my mother will wash away her sorrows while waiting to receive my father and me in the next life.

The Command Post

It was half-past four in the morning, another sleepless night wondering how I could convince my uncle not to turn me in to join the army.

The noise of a rumbling car engine, which sounded very close to the front door, kept me awake and alert until the sound stopped and was replaced by a loud banging on the metal door.

"Mr Sanday! Open up!" a thunderous voice boomed.

"I am coming," my uncle replied, as if he had been awake all night waiting for this signal. Alarmed, I sat upright on my sleeping floor mat. I heard my uncle open the door and an unfamiliar male voice ask, "Where is he? We must be quick, we are on a mission."

"Eba," called my uncle and, even before I answered, I knew it was the army.

He introduced me to the men who were dressed in full military uniform with a red band around their arm emblazoned with the two letters, 'MP'.

I watched with my own eyes as my father's half-brother handed me over to the military against my will, at a time when no one was proud to pick up arms for their country any longer. I saw Aunty Agnes, together with her children, standing on the veranda watching the incident unfold, but she did nothing. As for Gina, I saw her wiping some tears

THE COMMAND POST 29

that had appeared in the corners of her eyes.

The morning sun was coming up and the field was dusty when we arrived at the Armed Forces Command Post, the A.F.C. P, which was busy with young boys and girls of my age who were already in uniform and parading in the open field. They looked determined and carried automatic rifles during the exercise. Other recruiting companies were training separately on the same field, singing as they jogged several laps of the training field. Their team leader was at the front carrying a short, hard stick under his left armpit while the boys, with heavy and loud voices, sang a song.
"There is no mother here,
There is no father here,
We will train until we bleed."
The entire camp was busy with training activities. At the far side, near the bushes, was a firing range where the B Platoon carried out a firing exercise. The commander in charge of the camp which housed the 1st Crack Battalion, a colonel wearing a casual military T-shirt, camouflage pants and brown boots, was driving in a green open jeep on patrol, inspecting and evaluating the diverse training exercises.
'Train until you bleed' was the slogan of the armed forces. It was written boldly on the wall at the main entrance to the camp.
Our squad were the latest arrivals that morning, fresh and ready to be crucified and raised again to serve. We were received by a team of four military provosts headed by a lance corporal by the name of Caro, according to the nametag attached to his breast pocket. Corporal Caro had undoubtedly disciplined many field commission officers. I recognised the

merciless expression etched on his face. The provosts were well-dressed and wore blue bands around their arms. They commanded us to stand in two lines before they led us on foot toward the premises of our new training company. After a short march, we arrived in front of a large green tent where about fifty soldiers in uniform stood alert in long rows with their heads cleaned shaved. A sign read: 'D Company, here you are not welcome'. I glanced inside the tent and saw that it was full of camp bed stretchers, neatly installed in rows. Next to the beds were bags and other military equipment which looked as if they belonged to the soldiers who were housed there. The staff sergeant was a tall and tough looking soldier. We were asked to stand separately from the soldiers as the provosts handed us to the head of our recruiting team. His name was staff sergeant Njai, a tall and muscular man with a horseshoe moustache which was perfectly trimmed down to the corners of his lips. His moustache was so thick that I could barely see the shape of his upper lip. He had a square-shaped face structured with a strong jaw. His appearance gave me the impression that Njai was a seasoned carrier soldier. I didn't want to become one of his kind, even though I looked as if I already was. The staff sergeant, along with his team of four assistants, prepared a training plan while we waited. Everyone was quiet and focused. After a while, I heard voices and the sound of clicking boots. It was a team of twelve men from logistics, carrying equipment wrapped in transparent plastic bags which gave me the feeling that they were unused.

"Prepare to be cleaned up, you bloody civilians!" one short and old looking soldier from the logistics team commanded us. I was baffled because we hadn't received any orders since we'd arrived. My squad mates, equally bewildered, looked at each other stupidly.

"We are going to shave your heads to keep you clean for training," the soldier said, his voice cracking like thunder, "you boys stink." We were taken aside, asked to remove our clothes, and the logistics officers took out their shaving sets and began to do their job. I saw blood on a few heads after the shaving operation.

Green camouflage uniforms were supplied to us along with packages which contained an array of military gear, from berets to boots and backpacks. Once dressed, I felt like I had become a new man, in an image I disliked intensely. As we began to move to join the other recruits the cooking pan, cup and spoon hanging on my backpack made a ridiculous sound.

We were informed that our training would last for two weeks, and that upon completion we would be immediately deployed to the border front. Outside on the main training field staff sergeant Njai and his training team were ready to continue and we lined up to listen to their orders.

"Not one of you standing here is a fool," staff sergeant Njai began addressing the new recruits, "you boys are young, smart and fit. If any one of you considers themselves not to be fit I am here to make you believe." The staff sergeant looked serious as his searching eyes scanned us from where he stood above us on a small platform.

"From now on," Njai continued, "consider yourselves not as boys anymore but as men. Men who have taken vows and offered their lives and services to their fatherland. Be the one who will take the lead in this new struggle and make a difference. Today we will start preparing you to be physically and mentally fit. If you think you are not yet ripe to be picked, you better be now. Move!" he yelled.

That was how the training started. The whole company was taken to the forest and split into four platoons, each with its own commander, and tasked with cutting wood and learning forest survival skills. The following day we began our physical drills, which involved running long distances, crawling and hanging on ropes to cross obstacles. My muscles were tight and tangled due to the constant over-drilling by our instructors. It seemed like they wanted to fatten the pigs ready for market day. Two weeks to prepare a professional soldier was too short. The shortness of time meant the instructors pushed us at speed to, and beyond, our limits. At the time, the military needed more men as quickly as possible due to high tensions on the front.

On the fourth day of training, I made the decision to escape from the army training camp. That day was supposed to be the one on which we would touch a rifle and start our firing training.

It was three o'clock in the morning and everyone inside the tent was sleeping deeply, except me. My intention to escape filled my thoughts and precluded sleep. I wore my uniform under the bed cover to make easier for me, so I just had to put my boots on when the time came. Then I did what I had planned.

With a ghostly walk, I navigated through my comrades without disturbing anyone's sleep. When I stepped outside our tent, I was halted by the soldier on night guard, who happened to be one of my squad mates.

"Who goes there?" he asked.

"A friend."

"Where are you going, Eba?"

"To the latrine."

"Oh, duty calls, be careful, there are snakes out there at this time."

"I am a soldier," I addressed him confidently.

My escape was as smooth as the surface of a peeled boiled egg. Majestically I leapt on my toes and doubled my steps as I made my way into the bushes. I was thankful for the fact that there were no built latrines in the camp, and that everyone did their business alone in the nearest bush. I'd been told by one of my squad mates that escaping a military training camp can lead to serious consequences. One story which I'd heard recounted many times was that of a young soldier who had attempted to escape during a transfer trip and was shot dead in front of a market crowd where the convoy of recruited soldiers had stopped for shopping.

"He was shot from behind as he was desperately fleeing," explained my squad mate. Despite this story, and several other similar tales, I still made my move as I wasn't ready to stay in the army.

The forest was cold and foggy, but I knew the way and the training camp was not far from the town. We used to go into the forest to fetch dry wood and pick blackberries with boys from the area. Such trips were usually organised on Saturdays and although I wasn't a particularly welcomed guest to join the group I was fortunate to have Alimamy as a friend, and he always took me along.

After a two hour walk, the sky was still dark when I arrived at Alimamy's place as it wasn't yet dawn. The door to his room was still closed.

About a year earlier, just after he had turned seventeen, Alimamy had moved to a bigger town called Manga, where he lived independently in a tiny single room.

He had the freedom to choose for himself the things he wanted to do as he was raised by his real parents. Even after his move to Manga our friendship was still strong. I sometimes visited him in his tiny room where we spent time with schoolmates of his.

After I'd knocked several times on Alimamy's wooden door, he finally opened it wearing only his underwear, revealing his bare chest and a grumpy expression. He looked surprised to see me in a military uniform, and so early.

"May I come in?"

"I am sorry, you can't come in," he said, "I have a visitor in my room." He looked at me shyly and I understood him. I used to bring strangers to Alimamy's room too. The kind of strangers we both knew very well.

"What happened to you, Eba?"

"I was taken into the army against my will. My uncle turned me over. I don't want to sign up for service so I've come to you because I don't know where else to go. I need your help."

He looked up to the sky and nodded his head. "Walk with me to the backyard," he said.

Alimamy knew many people through his mother's restaurant. "Eba," he continued in a whisper, "you are in big trouble. I will direct you to a man who used to be a friend of my father. He helps many boys in your situation and he is against the idea of the regime forcing boys to join the army. His name is Karamokoh Dambay. He lives twelve miles away from here in a village he built for himself called Pameronkoh. You will be safe there and I believe he will help you find your way to some other place. Go quickly before the army find you here."

I took off my uniform and changed into civilian clothes which Alimamy gave to me. With his help, I dumped the uniform into the latrine and dipped it right into to the human waste with a long stick.

That early morning was the last time I saw my best friend. A true friend indeed.

A Prophecy

I footed the twelve-mile journey to Pameronkoh as fast as I could. The distance seemed much shorter because of the pace at which I walked.

My arrival at the self-built village of a traditional healer, who was also known to be a minority politician and a sympathiser of the masses, was a huge relief.

Karamokoh Dambay was renowned across the country for his talents in healing people using only natural herbs. His persistent effort in opposing the then ruling regime brought him to high esteem amongst local folks. His popularity exposed him to the dangers of the cruelty of the regime as they were always like a monkey on his back.

Karamokoh had already been locked up five times for opposing the ruling regime publicly. If it was true that the traditional healer was such a humanitarian, I would be pleased to meet him and to let him decide my fate.

The smell of boiling traditional herbs, even from a distance, was enough for me to recognise that I was in the territory of a healing sanctuary.

I passed many people who looked as though they had travelled from places even further away than I had. Wounded souls, hopeless, desperate and mentally ill people from all over the country came to Pameronkoh seeking solutions to their problems, and healing.

I felt the magic right from the first moment I shook hands with one of the finest traditional healers in the Continent of the Lions. From his handshake I got a strange sense that Karamokoh was somehow able to read my palm and look into my future.

He was a tiny man who looked to be in his late fifties, dressed in a long red gown, with his left leg wrapped around a walking stick which helped him to stand and walk properly. It seemed to me that one of his legs was disabled. He didn't have the charismatic personality I had imagined he would, but he came across as spontaneous and confident.

"What brings you here young man?" he asked, but before I could answer he ushered me inside hospitably.

He started talking before I had even introduced myself. "The spirits of your mother and father guided and led you here. You are a very lucky young man, here you can find the answers to many of the questions you have been asking yourself," he said, with no sense of humour. It is true that first impressions go a long way, and I was impressed by his first statement which somehow brought me to a state of belief. We went into a small hut, built of mud bricks just like all the other building in his village, where he served me some water from a clay water pot in a little calabash drinking cup.

"You don't need to explain much my son," he assured me when I attempted to introduce myself for the second time.

"I know who you are my son," he said, "the frog doesn't leave the hole during the daytime in vain." My mouth froze as he continued to preach.

"I know that the ancestors had met the Gods, and your fate

was already decided before you left your father's village. I only have to find out what destination you are heading to, when and how."

Goosebumps appeared on my skin and my mouth remained half open as if it had been filled with unwanted food. Karamokoh proceeded to tell more about my mother and father, including their names. From that moment, I concluded that I had finally met a living prophet.

"Tomorrow at full moon we will find out the answers to your future through the rituals," he said, as he started to show me around his house and into a small single room, which he offered me for the duration of my stay.

My body shivered as I sat on a low wooden bench, with four thick blankets covering me from head to foot. The smoke and cleaning ceremony, which lasted for two hours, was intense and suffocating. Between my legs stood an aluminium pot filled with natural and traditional herbs. Smoke rose from the pot and I felt the heat in my eyes and nostrils.

"Look at the smoke. Your future is bright, the leaves have answered your call. Many are called but few are chosen, and you are one of the chosen ones, Eba!" He laughed loudly and conferred with the other men who had helped with the process, who seemed to agree with him that the leaves had indeed answered.

The smell of assorted green herbs from the pot was strong and disturbing, and the heat from the boiling herbs made my whole body sweat so profusely that I looked as if I had just come out of a heavy rainfall. Karamokoh looked at me studiously and instructed me, "Go and have some rest, we will continue tomorrow." The process continued for three

days, before Karamokoh referred me to the next stage, and
left me feeling weak and tired. I was excited because, despite
having no idea of what was to come next, I believed that I
was in the hands of a man who could help me.

Under the bright and full moonlight I lay, on a mat made
from plastic, wondering how my uncle would react to my
escape from the training camp. Would he even care that the
Military Police were looking for me? I suspected not.

People crossed my path frequently as various rituals and
healing ceremonies took place simultaneously around the
sanctuary village.

One of Karamokoh's apprentices came to me with a message regarding the next ritual and the rest of the upcoming
process.

"You have to go inside the hut behind that tree, where
you'll find someone who will counsel you and give you more
information. That person is waiting for you, please hurry." A
huge, tall man, another of Karamokoh's aides, briefed me on
the next stage of the process.

When I looked from where I lay, I saw a small hut built
with sticks stuffed with red earth.

When I entered the hut, there was an old woman who was
busy boiling tea in a small pot made of clay, which sat on
top of three solid iron rocks with firewood burning underneath. She looked impatient and her body was noticeably
trembling.

"Welcome my son," the old woman whispered shakily,
"you are the one the bright forces were waiting for, although
you showed up a bit late it is better to be late than never," she
said with a little laugh.

Exhaustion after the smoke and cleaning ceremony held me back from responding to the old woman. My eyes were heavy, I longed only for a bed.

"Here is your tea." The old woman handed me a drinking cup full of hot, brown liquid. Steam swirled as it rose from the cup. My forehead was sweating and felt damp like the remains of the morning dew on the leaves during a dry season harvest. "Drink!" the old woman commanded me. "Drink from the finest of the most treasured herbs. It will make the words that come out of your mouth sweeter than honey, and your manhood stronger than iron or solid rock." The hot liquid hurt my throat after my first sip, and it took me a few minutes to adjust to the heat and finish drinking the tea.

The old woman's appearance reminded me of the story about the witch and the night watch. The deep wrinkles at the corner of her eyes were perfectly lined in the direction of her temples. Her eyes were shining in the dark like those of a lost cat in a nightmare and her mouth twisted down slightly to her chin, the chin of a vulture where she held a smoking pipe between her lips. Although her body was covered with a plain black cloth, I could see the tense veins on her forearms. In my imagination she transformed into the witch in the story. My thoughts wandered and I found myself considering the possibility that she was a witch. Witchcraft is a strongly held traditional belief in the land of Yougosoba, the land where my umbilical cord was buried. In the perspective of the common man in my country, anything negative that happened is said to relate to witchcraft, while any positive event is attributed to God's blessing.

It was already midnight when I left the old woman's tiny

hut. The moon was invisible and the blue velvet sky, which had shone three hours ago, had turned into a dark veil. I couldn't see anything in front of me and it seemed the entire sanctuary village was asleep. By the time I jumped onto my mat bedding I could wait no longer to rest my body and mind.

I was awakened by the sound of a cock crowing and the noisy clatter of aluminium pot covers from the kitchen. I was surprised to discover that I had gone to bed without underwear, wearing only the plain white cotton cloth which was wrapped around my body during the rituals. I looked like I was about to be put into my grave.

I greeted the chief medicine-man, "Good morning, Karamokoh." He looked confident in his long red gown and he held a rap of tobacco, which was still alight, clenched in the corner of his lips.

"You look fresh and ready to go young man. Last night I received a prophecy about your journey from the Gods, and they asked me to pass it on to you." He paused as he observed my reaction, which was not very welcoming. I was still struggling to come out of my usual early morning need for silence. My silence gave him the opportunity to proceed with his prophetic message from the Gods.

"There is a place called the Promised Land," he began, "it is situated at the south-east, but across the sea."

"Across the sea?" I asked, as my face divulged my dissatisfaction. He ignored me and continued. "The Gods have prepared you to go and recover a stolen treasure, which was stolen from our ancestors by men with silver blades, The Hundred Golden Horses." He referred to the treasure with an expression of vengeance before continuing. "The treasure was smuggled centuries ago and taken across the sea to the other side by some men who looked unwell and carried silver blades. I believe most of the stolen treasure was kept in the old underground city in the Promised Land. When you succeed in getting there, you will surely find a piece of treasure which legitimately belongs to you, Eba." He paused for a moment and looked at me intently before starting to speak again. "It will be a great stake of your inheritance. Go to the southern border and seek a man by the name of Jackie Blaak. He lives in a town called Blamba, he is a missionary of God who helps people like you. His life mission is to pave the way for those who have been forced to leave this land not from their own choice, but as a result of the fear, constant oppression and political detention manufactured by the present regime. I don't know Mr Blaak personally as a missionary, but I can trust him in spirit. I do believe he is a good man because I have sent a few victims to him and he has always helped them, a fact which makes me believe he can help you out of here and show you the way to the Promised Land where you will find your life changer." When he had finished speaking, he pointed his index finger in a southerly direction and cleared his throat. I had observed that usually when a man clears his throat it means that he wants to say something more, and this was no exception. Karamokoh continued his words of prophecy.

"In your case, the spirits warned me that you cannot afford to pay me right now, you are just a poor runaway boy, but we can strike a deal if you wish," he proposed.

"Yes sir, sure, I will do anything you wish, sir," I answered in a desperate voice.

"I can guarantee that you will succeed in going to the Promised Land and fetching back the treasure, I have no doubt about it. But I demand that you pay me back a fifty percent share of the value of the treasure you will find. You have to be honest with me when the time comes, otherwise my eyes will see beyond the seas and my hands will be long enough to reach you no matter where you are," he smiled and continued, this time in a more serious tone, "Eba, it is forbidden by the Gods for you to come back here with empty hands, without my share of that stolen treasure, and I guess you know what the consequences are going to be if you fail," he paused and looked intently at me, his eyes flickering a light red colour like flames.

"Yes, Karamokoh," I agreed.

"The moment you step foot on the soil of the Promised Land, everything will be alright, no more pain, no more sorrows. Misfortune will never stand in your way and success will be something you will enjoy for the rest of your life. After you leave this land you must remember that fifty percent will change your life, and mine, forever. Now go! Go to the Promised Land and find your stolen treasure," he shouted as he turned his back to me and started walking away. When I turned around to leave the village, I realised we had attracted the attention of the other patients. They stood beside their huts looking at me as if they were giving a farewell to the chosen son who has to leave for an adventure in search of a holy charm which can save the land from its bondage. Tears welled in my eyes as I had the feeling that I, Eba Yoko, the son of a farmer and a palm wine tapper, was about to sink into a new world. A world which I didn't know about but had to discover. I was apprehensive about the journey ahead and couldn't judge whether I was going to see the underworld or the true new world. Would it be like the stories my grandmother used to tell me about the fearful world, or be the real world which my late mother suffered to deliver me into?

After my farewell with Karamokoh, I went to the old woman's hut to say goodbye. She came out and kissed me on my forehead, and handed me a plastic wrap filled with a mix of gari, sugar and peanut butter. "Eat from it when you are hungry, it will keep you alive and help you remain strong on your journey." The old woman waved a farewell and returned into her tiny hut.

From that day, when Karamokoh had told me about the Hundred Golden Horses and the Promised Land, his prophecy gave me hope and became a new dream in my life. It was a goal I could have never dreamed of before I met him, yet I strongly believed it was going to become a reality. I left my land full of determination to return back home with a box full of treasure, like a knight coming home from war with a smile of fortune behind the trunk of his carriage.

A Journey Through Scorpions

It was a hot Wednesday afternoon when I arrived in the small town of Blamba near the southern border where I was to meet the missionary, Blaak.

In the distance I saw a small boy, who looked about eight years old, with a proud smile on his face. His body language was that of a sportsman who had just won a world championship trophy, and I wondered why he was smiling at me. He kept on smiling as we approached each other, until we were standing face to face in the middle of the dusty red earth road.

He wore orange swimming shorts and his bare upper body was shiny, as if he had just applied an oily tropical ointment to his skin. As he walked, his bared feet twisted a bit to the front and back, like those of a hunting lion.

"Who are you looking for?" he asked.

At first I was lost for words, suspicious that he seemed to know I was looking for someone, but within a split second I made up my mind to answer him.

"I am looking for a missionary, a man called Blaak," I told him.

"I know him, and I know where he lives. Sometimes he buys me fish cakes at the market, he is a good man," the boy continued talking as he led me to the missionary's house.

His hospitality made me believe that our Gods were travelling with me. As we walked, the boy voluntarily told me more about the man who was going to show me the way to the Promised Land.

From a few meters away I saw a middle-aged man wearing glasses with large, round, transparent lenses which gave his eyes an owl-like appearance.

"That's him," the boy said as we approached Blaak's house. The missionary was dressed in a plain black gown with pleated shoulder pads.

"Thank you for your kindness," I said to the boy who had led me there, and who I now regarded as an angel sent to help me out of the wilderness. A good Samaritan who appeared to me as a boy. A boy who had perhaps been raised in a good home, and to parents who taught him good values and the importance of showing hospitality to strangers. The boy made me think of my father who often advised me, "Son, you should always help strangers, then someone, someday, somewhere might help you when you have become a stranger too."

The boy left without saying goodbye. I saw him leaping on his way back into the wood. That was the first and last time I ever set eyes on that boy, even though I stayed for three days in his village. I thought about the boy often and regretted that I hadn't asked him what his name was.

The missionary introduced himself, "My name is Joseph Blaak. You are most welcome here. I was expecting you."

"My name is Eba Yoko."

"It is a pleasure meeting you Eba, for only the chosen seeker could find the humble helper."

"Can you help me reach the Promised Land, sir?" I asked

impatiently.

"Well, as the wise one said, you should take a good look at the sunset before you take an evening trip into the wilderness. You took a good look Eba Yoko, that is the reason why you made it here to my house."

"My gratitude, sir!" I replied, bowing my head a bit lower to the floor.

Mr Blaak invited me inside his house and took me to my lodging room. It was a large room with a king size bed. The atmosphere in the room was so welcoming that I knelt down and thanked God for giving me salvation.

My temporary bed was luxurious compared to my bed at my uncle's house. The bed I was going to sleep on for the next three nights appeared to be the most comfortable bed I had ever seen.

At my father's farm, I used to sleep on a bed made of sticks with a mattress made from the strain of thrashed rice plants.

The missionary's bungalow was painted white with transparent glass windows. The canopy in front of the main door was supported by ancient Roman pillars which gave the house an exotic appearance. It stood in an isolated area, surrounded by nature.

"You can stay here for the next three days," the missionary offered. I noted his modest way of dressing and his gentle demeanour and thought these things were unusual for a man of his status, and certainly a stark contrast to the way my uncle dressed and behaved.

I thought it unusual that in the land of Yougosoba a man with a great title, and living a luxurious life, was willing to offer such warm accommodation to a common boy like me, and I was grateful to have met such a person.

The heat was at its peak which drove me to retire to the garden to have some rest on the perfectly netted hammock tied between two apple trees. It was like lying in a little heaven, and when the breeze blew I thought a ripe apple might just fall onto my chest. I was almost falling asleep, after a few swings propelled by the cool afternoon breeze under the apple trees, when I felt something cold but alive softly licking my bare heels. I opened my eyes in dismay and shouted for help when I saw a big brown Leonberger, an unusual dog, standing next to me and panting from its opened mouth. In an acrobatic manner, I jumped down from the hammock as another dog of the same breed appeared and chased me with long sprints, its legs stretched wide. The scene we staged looked like a comical one of a dog chasing a cat.

"Somebody, help!" I yelled as both dogs pursued me as I ran around one of the trees. I heard an unexpected voice come out from nowhere.

"Hey!" the voice said, "Tinki and Striker, stop there right now!"

The dogs stopped at once. The man who had emerged from the pigsty to intervene looked like he was executing an SAS rescue operation, where a soldier missing in action is terrified and in desperate need of help. He wore a green overall and gloves.

"Don't be afraid of them, they won't bite you," he reassured me before introducing himself. "My name is Tamba."

I smiled at him, attempting to disguise my nervousness, and said, "I won't be. I am Eba." I stood perfectly still watching the two giant dogs, both laid flat on their forelegs beside Tamba, as they stared at me attentively with their ears straightened.

Tamba was one of the boys from the missionary's house.

My fear of dogs, in general, came from the many dog bites that had killed several people in front of my own eyes in my village.

During my childhood, people in our community didn't trust dogs. Dogs were not allowed to go near strangers or inside houses. But the missionary's dogs seemed to receive special treatment and were well trained. They were allowed to be with people just like any other human being. I immediately thought of Sembu's father, who hated dogs so much that, if a dog stepped on him by accident, he would chase it and make sure that he kicked it back even harder.

The following day, I took a dog training workshop from Mr Blaak which helped me to understand that his dogs were not a danger to me, but just wanted to be friends with me, and we did become good friends eventually.

"Prepare your baggage, we are leaving first thing tomorrow for the border," announced missionary Blaak.

I did exactly as he had instructed. I packed my bag with my underwear, clothes and other essential items, and carefully wrapped the remaining gari which the old woman from Karamokoh's village had given to me.

It was in my mind that I should eat from it only when I was hungry, which meant I should reserve most of it for the worst moments of hunger.

The missionary had warned me about my journey and given me some tips about the route we would be taking.

Though he didn't offer many details about the journey, and I did not dare to ask straight questions of such a powerful man who was about to help me out of servitude.

As the night passed by, I had fun playing with the dogs, Striker and Tinki. I knew they would both miss me when I was gone.

There was a huge transit centre at the southern border town of Saiul, which connects people to different routes across the region, where we arrived in heat. The temperature was above thirty degrees.

The crowded terrain was full of people from all over. Traders with small businesses coming from different cultures and places made it a busy and chaotic market place.

We were standing in the middle of the park when Blaak warned me, "This is a border town, take care of your belongings. Travellers often complain about their bags and wallets being stolen here."

His long black gown glittered under the sun. I wondered how he survived the heat with that gown covering him. I was in my short jeans and a white sleeveless shirt, but my muscles still felt the penetrating heat of the sun.

The missionary knew exactly where he must take me. He was relaxed, like any local on his own soil, and people greeted him warmly and respectfully as we walked by.

We entered a restaurant for lunch and I could barely contain my appetite when I caught the aroma of fried fish and cassava bread. The smells were delicious and reminded me of the food Alimamy's mother used to cook in her restaurant back home. At once I thought of my best friend and felt grounded.

"I am going to take you to the next town where you will join a group of other runaways. They will be your guide during your journey to the Promised Land," the missionary said to me as he chewed the last part of the Bonga fish which had been served with peppered sauce and cassava bread.

"But will you promise me one thing, Eba?" he asked.

"Just ask me, sir," I replied.

"Will you promise me that you will always pray before you eat anything during your journey?" I smiled, as if his question was irrelevant, and assured him, "Yes, I'll promise you, sir,"

It sounded like a promise a mother would ask of her child before leaving for a short holiday, and in his words I sensed something of my mother in the missionary.

During our conversation, a man came into the restaurant and greeted the missionary with sweaty hands. The two men seemed familiar with each other and spoke in a strange language which I had never heard before. Suddenly the atmosphere changed as the missionary's gentle tone changed into a more aggressive one and his facial expression appeared more serious than it had at the start of their conversation.

I saw a different missionary from the one I had met three days ago. On the other hand, I thought it was perhaps natural for someone to change their tone when speaking a different language which made me less concerned about the missionary's anger.

Within minutes we left the restaurant and headed towards four cars which were parked outside. I was wondering where we were going and whether the journey would take me to a place where I would be happy. I wondered whether the people inside the car were traders or ordinary travellers like me.

I had heard stories about a tribe from the north of our country who trade everything in exchange for money. I'd heard that those traders were so desperate for money that they even traded their own wives and children in exchange for things more precious to them.

I felt anxious but tried to control my nerves as the missionary and I got nearer to the cars. Neither my heavy backpack nor the plastic bottle of water in my hand could help me find the answers to the questions racing through my mind.

When I glanced into the cars, I was shocked by what I saw. People were crammed next to each other like herrings in a can. The space for them to breath was as narrow as a thread. When I lowered my nose a strong human odour evaporated like smoke from a dumping site.

"Welcome on-board ," a strange man greeted me.

I gave a hollow smile and thanked him, though my voice was trembling and I sounded like a radio with a battery that had almost run out.

"Get inside the car," the missionary instructed as he gently pushed my head toward the car. Although it wasn't a hard push, I was concerned about how the missionary handled my head. It was difficult to get into the car, which was already overloaded with people, and as I hesitated the missionary gripped my head, forcefully this time, and shoved me in. It was the car that the welcome voice had come from.

"Shift a bit everyone," the driver asked kindly. It was clear that I had no choice but to force my way into the back seat with my legs folded uncomfortably. I sat next to the man who had welcomed me. Next to him sat a heavily sweating man, clutching a holy rosary in his right hand, speaking silently to himself while he gently counted the little beads of the rosary in his fingers. He looked focused as he continued counting, muttering the numbers to himself under his breath. I wasn't sure what he was doing, but it looked like he was performing some sort of religious or traditional ritual.

The car engines hummed as they revved up. The drivers accelerated, sending a plume of dusty earth into the air.

The missionary and his friend got into one of the vehicles at the front. I heard the bang as he slammed the car door. The deliberate way he slammed it surprised me. It seemed to say 'I am in charge here'.

The doors of the brown Peugeot were not in good order and looked as if they could fall off as the men who sat next to them slammed them shut.

It was a rough six-hour ride through rocky hills with too many obstacles, including checkpoints in almost every village. Fortunately, everything appeared to have been arranged by the missionary and his friend at the front of the motorcade. As passengers, we had nothing to do but to stay in the car and wait until the missionary signalled the driver to move on.

We passed through the checkpoints smoothly. It seemed like a well-planned arrangement and we encountered no delays, or questions regarding our personal identification. One soldier just walked around the cars, lowering his head as he looked at our sweaty faces. I heard the missionary talking to the officials at the checkpoints, but I couldn't understand the language they communicated in and I admired the missionary as the first bilingual person I had met.

We finally arrived at our destination, which looked like a buffer zone surrounded by sand-covered hills.

There was no sign of a village or any indication of human existence. Neither was there a source of drinking water. The suspended, invisible heat felt like a religious leader had once described the heat from the gates of Hell, a heat that a sinner's remains would have to endure for the rest of their time in their graves before they faced their final punishment after the day of judgment.

"Listen up everyone!" said the missionary's friend.

"From here and now on," he said, "all of you should consider yourselves as birds that have to survive flying across this desert to reach the Promised Land. Some of you will make it, and others will not. Pray. Use every charm you are carrying with you. Use your physical body if you want to survive this journey. Going back is not an option, as the way back is already closed. Your life, your destiny, is now in the hands of one man, and that man is me. The journey will be easier for those of you who are ready to obey my orders," he ended, sweating under the burning sun. There was a moment of silence before the murmuring began.

"Yes, no turning back!" I was surprised when I realised that chant came from one of three men who had appeared from nowhere. I hadn't heard any footsteps or any signal to indicate that someone was coming. The men were dressed in peculiar traditional clothing. Each wore a long blue gown with a broad golden coloured leather belt tied around their belly, braced with a silver metal buckle. I couldn't see the colour of their hair due to the white thick turbans wrapped on their heads, which also partially obscured their faces. They were accompanied by three strange animals, with long necks, tall skinny legs and hunchbacks, which they had brought to carry our baggage.

I turned around and looked at the faces of the newcomers to see if I could make eye contact, but there was nothing. The missionary climbed into one of the cars which was already pointing in the direction we had come from, then the other drivers got into their respective cars and made U-turns.

I shed a tear as the missionary left me, in the hands of strangers, in the middle of nowhere.

I was frightened. I thought about the stories I'd heard about cannibalism and, from that moment on, things started to turn around.

I remembered something a stranger had once told me, 'Whenever a man travels to a strange land he automatically becomes a little child'.

Remembering the stranger's words brought me to the realisation that I was the traveller and it would be wise for me to seek advice from, and listen to, the natives. My heart told me, 'Obey and comply, you will be spared,' and I repeated that to myself silently. 'Obey and comply, you will be spared.'

That thought became my guiding principle throughout my journey.

The Desert Storm

The temperature dropped progressively as we continued our journey east on foot, which helped us to stretch our legs and flex our muscles after the long and bumpy car ride to the desert.

Bags were packed with food, tents, and other essentials and loaded on to the backs of the animals. They moved slowly, weighed down by all the baggage they carried. They were the slowest animals I had ever seen.

Curious, I took a few steps toward the cargo and asked one of the men dressed in white traditional clothing with a turban wrapped around his head, "Excuse me, sir. What animals are they?"

The man turned around, looked at me straight into my eyes and, without a word, turned again and continued walking. There was a little murmuring going on at the back, but I was the first person in the group who had dared to ask a question of the native. I felt ashamed of myself as my question had been ignored by the desert man, a man who looked physically weaker than me, but I told myself it didn't matter and walked away from him.

From a distance, I heard the crows of strange birds. The sound became louder as we got closer and I saw a fleet of white birds in the sky, suspended in one position. The birds looked like seagulls or birds of prey from a distance and I imagined them feasting on an animal carcass. My thoughts were interrupted by a voice, "Listen up everyone," our group leader said, "we are approaching the falls of Zamzam. When we reach the falls, we will take a break to drink and eat something. But beware of one thing, this place attracts many different species and we could encounter all kinds of predators who inhabit this part of the desert. So, be prepared for the unexpected." Once more, my whole body was consumed by fear as he spoke.

A man beside me said, in a sarcastic manner, "Now the true journey has begun. Let real men demonstrate their true strength."

My preoccupation with quenching my thirst was increasing rapidly. Fortunately, as we neared the area where the birds were clustering, I heard the sound of a waterfall starting to whisper in my ears. It sounded like we were approaching signs of life. And I mean the true source of life. Water.

With relief, I smiled at the desert man. He was the leader of the team of three men who were in charge of our baggage and the animals.

After a slight hesitation, he smiled back at me and I was pleased by his response, as that was the first time I had seen a desert man smiling. For me, smiles are important because they are always profitable. When I was a little boy I used to smile a lot, and I still do.

"Baggage controllers hold on tight to your animals. It seems there is a little trouble ahead of us," our group leader announced.

When I lifted my eyes I saw that we were standing a few meters away from the waterfall and I gasped in admiration. The waterfall, and its surroundings, looked like paradise in the middle of the desert.

I realised that nature is far smarter than people think. Someone who had not been here could surely never imagine it was possible to find a waterfall in the middle of the desert.

Mesmerised by the waterfall's natural beauty, I found myself imagining another world and momentarily lost myself into a dream inspired by my appreciation of the beautiful surroundings.

When I returned to my senses, I turned my eyes to the left and realised that everyone in the group was staring at me.

At first, I didn't get it.

"Is everything ok?" I asked.

The desert man alerted my attention by pointing to my right. When I turned around to see what he was pointing at, I saw a pride of desert lions quenching their thirst at the base of the waterfall. It looked as if they had just finished their last meal of the day.

I was used to seeing lions in my village, but never as close as that.

In rare cases, lions had attacked people in the jungle where I was born.

As I was about to ask another question, the group leader put his finger to his lips as a sign we should keep quiet and not move. I was familiar with this gesture, an unspoken language I understood well from the war in my country, when adults would signal to their children while hiding during an attack.

The birds were still flying above our heads and in that moment it seemed as if the humans and birds had the same plight, with both groups holding back in recognition of the dominance of the kings of the desert.

After five minutes of fearful silence, three lion cubs arrived. They were lively and wrestled brutally with each other, punching each other with their sharp claws like young boxing stars demonstrating their skill and their ambition to become heavyweight champions in the future. They looked innocent and cute to me, but maybe not to my fellow travellers.

The young stars' activity, as they jumped around and let out little cries, aroused the attention of their parents and the whole group of lions turned and marched majestically in the direction the cubs had come from. Slowly, they vanished into the wilderness.

When the lions had gone, everyone breathed a sigh of relief and visibly relaxed. As our fear subsided a few were still mouthing prayers. I noticed the different demonstrations made by my fellow travellers to show a sign of thanksgiving to their Gods for saving them from the situation. The scene looked like a little shrine, where people from differing belief systems would meet and perform their rituals to achieve a common goal.

"This is what I talked about," the group leader said arrogantly, "it is extremely dangerous out here in the desert. I'll warn you once more, you must listen carefully and use your head." I wasn't impressed by him, as he had only started speaking again after the lions were long gone. The incident reinforced my opinion that the lion is the king of the desert and jungle.

As we moved forward to drink, the shallow part at the base of the waterfall was quickly occupied by a fleet of different birds and little reptiles who, like us, had waited patiently for the lions to leave. The birds and mammals were desperate as they tried to scare each other away to secure a comfortable drinking territory. We waited for the birds to leave, just as they had waited for the lions.

As someone born in an environment rich with nature, I had hoped a time like this would come, when humans would make way for animals and nature and give them a chance of survival.

The evening sky was seductive as the pale, orange-tinted colour slowly dissipated in the atmosphere. At sunset, the birds and mammals finally left the plunge basin of the waterfall. I hoped and prayed that another group of wild animals wouldn't show up, as if that happened our group would become the waterfall's night watchmen.

I was relieved and refreshed as I quenched my thirst at the shallow side of the waterfall. The water was so crystal-clear you could see the sand underneath, and it smelled fresh and clean compared to the unsanitary conditions of the river water I was used to back home.

Some of the travellers immersed themselves in the water, stripping naked and swimming into the depths of the lake. I didn't dare to do so, still afraid of what I had seen at the waterfall. I was determined to stay alert and not to lose myself, not even for a moment.

After a brief respite at the water, it was time for us to cross over to the other side. The lake was about fifty meters wide, underneath the waterfall hundreds of meters high, but it was shallow enough for us to wade across and the water only came up to our knees.

We walked for another mile before taking a break. "We will spend the night here," announced our leader. It was a sandy field, the size of two football pitches. Most of the land was flat, but from the east low hills were formed by shiny, golden sand.

The baggage carriers offloaded the baggage from the animals' haunches, taking some firewood to set a camp fire, while the rest of us were busy preparing the sleeping tents. I was excused from helping to set up the camp, probably because I was the youngest and most inexperienced amongst our group.

I focused my attention on our group leader, watching what he was up to.

He held a map in his hand which he studied intently. He had a walkie talkie radio handset which he spoke into regularly.

After setting up the camp, our leader divided us into four groups of four people, each group had their own tent.

It was already dark, though the moon shone brightly above us. The magic of the night was the twinkling stars in the dark sky. The atmosphere was quiet and peaceful, and various different species of glowing insects flew around us. Even though we were in the middle of a tedious journey, it felt like we were a highly honoured convoy of diplomats spending the night in a five-star hotel in the middle of a fabulous desert city.

The desert man set a fire and started roasting some meat, already seasoned with hot chillies and spices, which emitted a strong and tantalising aroma. As he prepared the food, the others busied themselves performing their evening religious rituals. It appeared to me as if most of the travellers' minds were occupied by different beliefs, which I thought was a good sign as perhaps I would be saved one day by another man's prayers.

My uncle used to tell me, "Prayers change things," but I still didn't know how things could be changed through prayers. At that time I only believed that prayers could bring hope to people during desperate times in their lives.

I had observed that my uncle was a man who believed things which he had never seen with his own eyes, and that some of those things would become serious problems in the lives of the people he forcefully converted to believe. For me, the issue of faith appeared to be questionable, as I was still young and had a lot to learn about life in general.

It was getting late and people had started moving into their tents. I lay on the sand outside our tent looking up at the beautiful sky.

The desert man came close to me and asked, "What is your name, son?"

"Eba," I answered quietly.

"You are not afraid," he said, "people can only survive the desert if they can overcome the common enemy, their fear.

Your worst enemy is the fear that lives within you. But you, Eba, you are strong." He winked at me, a sign which reassured me that everything was all right between us.

After my first conversation with the desert man, I remembered a woman who had once told me that I was strong like my mother, but what always bothered me was that I didn't have an image in my mind of what my mother really looked like.

When my thoughts of my mother subsided, I sat up with my legs folded, as the desert man had been seated for the whole evening, and he put his hands on my cheeks, looked into my eyes and whispered in my ear, "Don't be frightened, I am here for you. I will protect you. Look at me and imagine that someone from your village is holding you right now." He let go of my face and I felt a rush of emotion. After a short silence, I stood up and went into my tent without saying a word.

With three other people already inside the tent it was hot and uncomfortable. I laid down on the floor mat with the others. Again, I started thinking about my grass mattress bed made of dry harvested rice straw which I slept on for most of my childhood years at my father's house. Since I left with my uncle, I didn't know whether someone else had taken over my childhood bed or not. During all those years I spent at my uncle's house, I rarely heard from my father and it was possible that during those silent years someone else was sleeping in my bed, perhaps even a little brother or sister. I felt homesick again as I thought about my friends, my little radio, the farm lands, the sheep and the chickens. I missed the landscape and, above all, the Alligator River.

Before I fell asleep, people were already snoring in their tents. It sounded horrible, different sounds at different paces, some of them were high and some were low but sharp like a whistle. I couldn't sleep. My body was cold and my mind was racing with strange thoughts. I wondered whether the lions would come and attack the camp. At that moment, I heard a sound like a rocket whistling and it kept coming closer to my ears. The tent started shaking as the sharp sound and vibration I'd heard initially intensified with every second. I realised it was a violent storm. I woke the others up and braced myself as the storm's strength increased and hit harder, as if the Gods of the storm were angry with the way the earth was mishandled by its own inhabitants. The whistling sound of the angry wind was something I had never encountered before. Afraid, I wondered if doomsday was here. That was how people in Looking Town, where I was raised, used to describe it when nature took its course.

Within a few moments, everyone had woken up and was holding on tightly to the tent as the violent storm threatened to uproot the ropes it was secured with. We battled to hold on as firmly as we could, waiting for nature to decide what it wanted to do with us. One man looked terrified and started performing his ritual with his rosary as the storm continued to hit hard as it progressed to its climax.

I heard things crashing into the tent from outside, though I didn't know what they were. Inside the tent I could see my fellow travellers' terrified expressions and my whole body was shaking for what was, at that point in my life, the scariest thirty minutes I had endured.

Finally, the catastrophic storm gave way to an eerie quiet. I carefully drew up the zip that secured the entrance of our tent and looked out, waiting for a sign of movement. Everything was still, which gave me the courage to open the tent and step outside. It was a mess. I saw our baggage had been thrown around in the wind and had landed in awkward positions.

The desert man came out of his tent, followed by our group leader, and started picking up things and putting them back in order.

"What are you doing outside?" our leader asked.

"I just came to help with clearing the mess."

"That is not your task," he replied angrily.

I ran quickly back into my tent and joined my sleep mates. "It seems as if someone is trying to interfere with the boss's business," I muttered in amusement.

Inside the tent people were already snoring again, which surprised me given it was just a moment since the terrific storm, and I joined the party when, unable to stay awake, I too fell into sleep.

When I opened my eyes, it was daylight again. I heard sounds of rumbling groans which I assumed was from the animals. The loud voices of my chatting fellow travellers encouraged me to get up at once.

I was the only person still asleep inside the tent. It seemed the people I was travelling with were early birds.

I wondered what would have happened if the group had

left me there and continued their journey without me, but I tried to stop myself considering that possibility too much as it was a dream full of nightmares.

I was delighted by the beautiful sunrise, which looked like a coloured bulb hanging on the horizon.

When I stepped out of the tent, the first thing I set eyes on was the desert man and his colleagues who were busy loading the baggage onto the back of the animals.

I approached him and said, "Good morning." He gave me a slanted look and said nothing in reply. He was a man who communicated more with his eyes than his words. In my village, it is a strong tradition for juniors to greet older people, especially in the morning. But some people don't like it, particularly when it is still very early in the morning. I thought that might be the case here with the desert man, who seemed to keep his distance from me.

I took a walk around the camp making connections with other travellers while they were busy folding up their tents. Our leader was busy communicating on his handset. "It was a sand storm at zero," I heard him saying to someone on the radio. Sometimes during our journey through the desert, I reflected on the attitude of our group leader, who was difficult to read. I wondered how such a short and small man could be in charge of not only me, but also of such a tedious journey. I considered that he may be a wise and well-connected man which would give him licence to become such an important person.

I noticed that two travellers in our group were wrestling violently in the middle of the desert while our leader was talking on his handset. The men, equal in height, were violently throwing blows at each other's faces. Blood from their noses spilled out before the gunshots went off. The two gunshots that separated the fighters came from a light pistol in the hand of our leader. Its tube pointed in the air as light smoke swirled up, and it smelled strongly of gun powder.

"You two, stop it!" he ordered after pulling the trigger, "I don't want to see this happen here anymore. I won't warn you again. Next time I will just do what I have to do if I see such behaviour."

Our leader had a gun. I then realised where his power lay, as a man with a gun in his hand always has the greatest opportunity to be in control.

"Pack up! Fold up!" our leader yelled. "We are moving north. Beware, there are desert scorpions along the way, they could sting you right into your bone. The poison they inject can cause a serious negative reaction quickly, especially during this season." He bent down, grabbed his boots laces and began to tighten them up. His black boots were so well-polished and shiny that you could see the reflection of your face in them.

I had no clue how the other travellers in the group were finding this experience, but for me that journey was my first travelling adventure. It seemed to me that the world was about to teach me new things. Things that I would have to pass on to my own future generation. Not knowing exactly where that journey would take us made me feel like I was hanging on a rope to cross a river inhabited by deadly crocodiles, on a mission to catch up with a group of runaway treasure thieves on the other side. A treasure which I had never laid eyes on, nor witnessed its robbery, but had vowed to bring back home half of its value as pay back to Karamo-koh Dambay. I had made an oath.

After the warning from our group leader, all our baggage was packed on the back of the three animals and we started moving north, under the shining sun.

I stayed close to the desert man because he had shown me a friendly face the previous day.

We walked side by side with the cargo carriers. They were speaking to each other in their own language, a language which was strange to me such that I couldn't understand a single word they said.

I attracted the attention of the desert man and asked him, "What animals are they?"

"They are camels," he said, "they can run sixty-five kilometres per hour and can drink fifty-two gallons of water in three minutes if there is an abundance. But remember, humans must drink first. These animals can survive the desert for a long period of time without eating a proper meal, and can also eat anything including your shoes in the worst situation. So, do not ever feed a camel with your last meal, especially in the desert, otherwise you will be watching him chewing while he watches you starve to death in the desert." He concluded with a genuine smile which I returned and told him, "Good to know."

"You can always learn by being a good listener my friend."

It seemed as if we were playing a game of words.

One of the other baggage men snatched the desert man's attention, calling him over for a short talk. After their conversation, he turned back to me and threw another question.

"Anyway, what is your name again, son?"

"Eba Yoko," I answered proudly. This time I included my family name and told him, "I was named after my great grandfather who was a warrior during the uprising against the occupation of the early royal empire in my country. My father used to tell me stories about him. My father said he was a strong man, though people thought he was an ugly looking man. I felt ashamed when my father told me that, but on the other hand I was proud of who my grandfather was."

"That makes him a unique gentleman," he replied, "as a matter of fact, what difference does it make if someone is ugly? Ugly people, as they are called, are also unique."

He took my arm and stood still with me, while the rest of the convoy kept moving forward.

Where we stood, he introduced himself to me in an official and formidable manner.

"My name is Samir El Sheik," he said, "I was born somewhere in the surroundings of this desert. My father used to be a desert warrior and taught me how to operate firearms and to trade with other people in this life. I am Samir, this is my life. If you play games with my daily bread, I will eat yours too." He looked at me straight into my eyes. His eyes were sharp and filled with tears. When I looked into his eyes it seemed as if I could see into his soul, which I sensed was a wounded one.

"Let's hurry and catch up with the others," he urged. We quickened our pace to close the gap between us and the rest of the group.

The other travellers were talking to each other as we proceeded towards the lower north of the desert, although the social contact within the group ebbed noticeably during the last few hours of our journey. It seemed as if everyone was busy making a new friend, or already had one, with the exception of our group leader whose only friends seemed to be his radio set and the map he carried.

The sound of roaring cars engines in the distance indicated to me that we were approaching another town, and my hopes were raised. I thought we were finally going back to normal life, to meet new people, but it later appeared to be something different. As we got closer to the engine sound I saw it was a motorcade of pickup trucks, all painted white and full of heavily armed men. The men were in a different kind of military camouflage. Uniforms and weapons that I had never seen during the war in my country. I was worried that they had come to interrogate us, but luckily the motorcade continued its way to the other side of the sandy road without stopping or saying a word to us.

"They call themselves the Army of Salvation," said Samir, "and they are busy fighting their own war." Changing the topic he said, "I want you to know one thing, Eba. Politics and religion are the two main factors which ignite most of the problems in this region. There is no hope for ordinary people, the foundation of the next generation is ruined. I believe it will be a generation which is driven only by hate. They will hate each other because love is something they will never experience."

His facial expression was bitter. I raised my head and said to him, "I experienced war when I was a little boy. I lost my mother during the curse of the war while I was just a baby. As I grew up I witnessed more of the war, and some of my friends were forcefully taken away to be recruited as child soldiers against their will. I still have to deal with the post-trauma stress because of the things I witnessed during the war, which have left their wounds and often give me nightmares."

"That must be tough for you, Eba," said Samir, "I can't imagine all the things you must have been through. My father once told me he was taken away to fight a war overseas when he was just sixteen years old. He used to shout and cry frequently during his sleep. He told similar stories to the one you just told me. My grandfather always told me I should never support a war because the worst situation in times of peace could be the best during wartime. But since I gained my self-consciousness as a human being, I have realised there has always been wars around the globe. I am looking forward to seeing the day of an international ceasefire, just one day on which not a single gunshot will be heard in any corner of this beautiful planet." Samir stopped talking and we observed a moment of silent

"That will be judgment day," I responded.

"Certainly it will be, Eba, but I don't see it forthcoming."

The Abandoned City

I heard the sounds of machines and car horns as we approached the city and, as we got closer, the voices of people speaking loudly. I sensed we were in a quite different environment than the one in which I had been raised, and I concluded that we had reached the Promised Land.

Before I settled down, the voice of our group leader emerged from nowhere.

"Listen up everybody! We are now approaching the abandoned city. This is a place where humans can be treated in any manner. There is no law and order here, nor is there mercy for the weak or poor. This is a city that has been abandoned by the international community because its previous leadership didn't respect the regulations of the new world order. This place is not a country anymore, it has become the centre of an experiment where various powers come to test their military might. In this city, the strong survive and the weak perish. My main goal is for each and every one in this group to survive the terrible challenges people face daily here. I demand your attention as I explain the rules of this city." He started to count.

"Rule number one," he began, "never talk to someone you don't know without my consent." He continued through the rest of the rules before concluding, "this place is the gateway to your freedom. This is the gateway to the Promised Land."

The end of his speech sounded like a well-written national assembly address. The fibres of emotion which evaporated from his speech brought half the group to tears, while the others rewarded him with warm applause for his brilliance, before we continued, in silence again, on the half a mile walk into the main city.

During the walk, due to extreme tiredness, I was looking down at my feet rather than at the path ahead and I clumsily fell into a small muddy hole which held my heels for a moment. When I freed myself from the mud my next step landed me in the abandoned city. I had no clue what was going on and was completely disoriented by the area and its activities. For the locals, it seemed like a normal route to walk on the muddy roads in the abandoned city.

Struggling to regain my orientation, I heard one of the travellers say, "This is the world of apes, a world where every child has to jump for themselves." His face made a little gesture of excitement after his contribution.

When I turned around to see who it was, I saw the nervous man busy counting the nubs on his rosary with his fingers. Only the good Lord knows in what ancient language he recited, but this time he looked happier than I'd seen him before.

For a reason which I couldn't clearly explain, I had become moody since our arrival in the abandoned city. It started when I began to feel a sharp pain in my muscles and on my spinal cord, a suffering which I believed was due to our long journey on foot.

"You little monkey!" our team leader yelled, pointing his finger straight at me. "You, follow that man standing next to you."

The man standing next to me was Samir, the desert man. I stared at him and he gave me a pleasant smile, but I knew it wasn't a sincere one.

The group leader dispatched the rest of the travellers to join strangers who were awaiting our arrival at the spot where we had gathered. The presence of the strangers reminded me of the fish traders in Looking Town, as they waited patiently at the wharf all day for the fishing boats to return from the sea. Then they would buy the day's catches and sell them at markets in bigger towns. At the time, it looked like a mutually beneficial arrangement, and both the traders and fisherman seemed satisfied with the deal. The plan of handing us over to the strangers, at least as far as I could remember, wasn't mentioned to me by the missionary, or by Karamokoh Dambay.

Our team leader wished us good luck and left. Samir handed the camels to a newcomer and asked me to go with him to his house.

On our way, I saw groups of petty traders along the narrow streets as I followed Samir. He didn't say a word to me, or to any other person, along the way. Samir hadn't told me any details about what was going to happen next, or where exactly we were heading to, and my enthusiasm for asking questions was long gone. I sensed that the atmosphere had become tense. On the streets I heard several strange languages and saw child beggars among the crowds of people from all kinds of races. It looked like the way my uncle had once described to me what judgement day would look like, with young and old, mothers and children, carrying their own load on their backs.

We arrived at a less busy street, paved with grey granite stones and lined with elegant houses. Samir stopped and knocked on the main gate of one of them. It was a red, two-storey building ventilated with transparent glass windows on the first floor, the second floor was sealed without windows. A man peeped out through a hole in the gate before opening it widely. It made a heavy rumbling sound as it opened and the gateman, closely followed by two others, approached us.

Samir and the gateman hugged each other with big smiles on their faces. They both looked relaxed as they greeted each other and the other men. Samir and I were received honourably by his men. In my eyes, he was received like a king who has just returned to his home town after a great triumph on the battlefield.

I saw loyalty in the eyes of his friends and it was clear they were already in a celebratory mood.

Samir welcomed me into the house and asked a woman to show me around and prepare me something to eat and drink.

The atmosphere during our arrival was warm and friendly. The woman Samir had asked to take care of me gave me the best hospitality that I had ever received from anyone in my young life. She was a shy woman with a small, innocent face. Her facial expression gave away something of her nature and I sensed that she was a good person. When she served me, she didn't dare to look at me in the face.

According to my tradition, a guest's length of stay depends on the manner in which they are first received and welcomed by their host. In our culture, an unwelcome guest would never be asked outright to leave, as nobody would want to be accused of throwing a guest out directly, but they would be indirectly asked to leave through their host's unwelcoming behaviour. My Aunty Agnes, as an example, was very good at kicking people out of the house. When they had an unwelcome guest, she would not talk to them much and she would never show the guest to their sleeping place on their arrival. Instead, she would stay up until Uncle Sanday came home in the late hours of the night, when my uncle would usually talk more with the guest and finally show them to their accommodation, by which time the guest would be exhausted after a long day.

Whenever I witnessed such events happening at my uncle's house, I would say under my breath, "Guest, you are not welcome here." But I never said it out loud, I wouldn't dare to, even in the absence of Aunty Agnes.

When night fell at Samir's, I went early to bed. I was physically and mentally exhausted and desperately longed to have some rest in the little single room which was illuminated by a slim white candle. The burning candle was dripping and the drops of wax looked like tears. Perhaps they represented the tears shed by the person who had lit it before I entered the room. The tiny room had concrete walls and no window. When I scanned around, I saw one ventilation space with three little bricks laid vertically, separated by narrow spaces in between. Through these spaces a little bit of fresh air managed to escape and make contact with my nostrils. The ventilation was installed only on one side of the wall. The steel door, painted red, had a big lock on the outside with two huge padlocks hanging from it, with keys in them. When I stepped into the room, I felt like I was entering a prison cell.

Despite suffering from the worst fatigue I had experienced on our journey so far, I struggled to fall asleep. My eyes were closed as I lay on the foam mattress, but my head was busily occupied with thoughts which overpowered the good angel who usually brought my deep slumber. For a few minutes I wasn't sure whether I was awake or asleep. The foam mattress, although it was laid on the bare floor without a bed cover, brought me some comfort and eventually I drowned into the world of my dreams.

Deep in my sleep I heard a voice whispering, close and clear, into my left ear. Again, I wasn't sure whether I was awake or asleep and dreaming. I had experienced something similar the night before I had escaped from the army. I had heard a voice whispering to me, "It is time for you to go, Eba." When I woke up the night before my escape I realised the voice that had spoken to me was my inner voice. But this time, at Samir's house, it was confusing as in my dream I heard two voices saying the same thing at the same time. The voice I'd heard in my dream at the army training camp was clear to me, but the other voice sounded strange and I was sure I had never heard that whispering voice before. When I opened my eyes, waking from the confusion, the room was completely dark as the candle had burned out. In a split second, there was a spark as someone turned on a sharp light. I heard the click of the switch on the flashlight. The light glittered in a way I hadn't seen before as it pointed straight into my face, still and focused on me such that I couldn't see who stood behind it.

"I won the bid and paid the cost of your worth. I paid your price, not only in kind but also in cash, and now you belong to me, Eba," said a voice behind the light.

My body shivered at his words, as if I'd received an electric shock. I still couldn't see the face of the person who spoke in the darkness and I didn't recognise the devilish voice, though it was a man's voice.

"Who are you?" I asked weakly.

"I am Samir, Samir El Sheik, your friend," he replied. "You had already been sold to me before we met in the desert. This place is my house and you have to follow my orders. In the desert, I was disguised as an ordinary baggage carrier but here I am a king." He stared at me arrogantly and advised, "If you are wise you will do whatever I ask you to."

My whole body started to shake in disbelief as I struggled to overcome a terror which I thought would defeat me.

"Look," he said, "you are the only reason I travelled all those miles through those deadly scorpions in the desert. You are my trophy, Eba, my catch of the day."

"I am not your trophy!" I cried out, in the same way I had done the day my uncle handed me over to the army.

At that moment, I realised I had been sold by someone, I had no idea who, for money. Even in my worst nightmares I had never imagined that I could one day find myself in a situation as terrible as this.

"This is the twenty-first century," I said to myself doubtfully.

Samir sounded aggressive and I realised, for the first time, that he may have a motive to attack me. Samir El Sheik, the desert man, a man who I thought of as my friend, rushed forward to grip my defiant hands and, when I resisted, pushed me violently against the wall. I stood up shakily and asked him what he was doing. He stared at me with cold eyes while the light laying on the floor flashed on his face. Pulling a gun from the back of his trousers, he pointed it at my forehead and hissed, "If you resist me one more time Eba, believe me, I will shoot you."

In any battle, the man with a gun in his hands always has the advantage over the unarmed, and my strength was broken by the fear of his weapon. Samir wasn't stronger than me physically, but my fear of being overpowered, tortured or even killed by him or his men gave him the upper hand. He won the battle. He held me at gunpoint and commanded me to take off my clothes before pouring an oily ointment on my behind and forcefully penetrating me. Groaning and panting like a beast he took away my innocence over and over again. The pain I felt at that moment was both physically and psychologically damaging, and would have killed me had I not been born a true man.

When I woke up the next morning, my pants were wet at the back and front.

I could feel a sharp pain from the scratch marks left by his uncut fingernails. The evidence of what had happened to me was visible all over my face in my shame of myself as well as on my body. I couldn't comprehend what Samir had done to me. A man who I had once thought of as my friend had become a predator worse than any in my nightmares.

The door opened and the woman who had offered me hospitality the previous day came in, wearing a blue and yellow unstitched sari dress draped over her body down to her feet which dragged behind her as she walked. I couldn't make out what colour her hair was as her head was covered with a black hijab.

She brought some bread with butter for my breakfast and left the room without saying a word. I wondered why she behaved that way. I'd hoped to share a comforting word or two with her, a conversation with someone was what I craved after the events of the previous night, but it didn't happen and my world continued to fall apart in silence.

The breakfast looked delicious, but I couldn't eat anything. I had no appetite. It seemed like during the day I was treated like a guest in a five-star hotel, but at night I would become nothing but a captive. That is how it continued every single day and night for the rest of the time I spent locked up inside that little hole.

I hadn't been allowed to leave the room since the night I entered its horrors. I even had to do my business in an old bucket which one of Samir's guards came to empty. At least that made me feel honoured like a king, as during the days of the empire when my great ancestors ruled it was an honour for an able-bodied man to arrive every morning to empty someone's excrement.

During my time in that civilised prison, Samir extended his acts of cruelty even further, to the extent that he brought in some pathetic, sick pleasure seekers who, with his permission, forced me to kneel and suck all the fat out of their hanging pipes. The pleasure seekers' arrogance convinced me that they had paid Samir for what they described as their 'special treatment'.

In the absence of any other choices, I unwillingly sucked many of those hanging pipes under fat bellies until I finally decided that enough was enough. That day when Samir came into the room I said to him, "If any of those men come up here and ask me to do such an act again, I swear I am going to bite that hanging flesh of theirs until I cut it off." I spoke with a desperate voice. "If you just try it again, you will see." From that moment the men stopped coming.

One morning when the woman brought my breakfast, she looked at me directly into my eyes. It was the first time she had dared to do so. Her face looked innocent and she tried to hold back light tears which were forming in the corner of her eyes. She reached into her bosom with her right hand and pulled out a folded piece of paper, which she gently handed to me. Without warning, she kissed me on my forehead and I felt the softness of her lips. Then, without a word, she left the room.

I was curious about whether it was a letter or just a grocery list, and impatiently unfolded the scrap piece of paper to read it.

Dear Samir,
Ten years ago, I was so thankful that my parents chose you to be my legally wedded husband. But when I got to know you better I realised that I agreed to marry you because I was naive and was pressurised by my parents to do so. Now I realise that I made the wrong decision. I cannot stay to witness the place I dreamed of, my matrimonial home, being turned into a slaughterhouse. I

wish I had met a man who could have provided the right liquid to fill my empty cup of desires, but you are not to be that one. You are a monster with many heads who I tried, but failed, to help.

I deeply regret marrying you. I will never forgive you or my parents for putting me into such a bloody plot. There is blood all over this place.

I believe I am not even blessed by God to conceive a child with you. Because of your wicked ways, God has cursed us. May he have no mercy on you.

I have prepared your dinner, which you will find ready on the dining table. Eat as much as you can, for you will never taste the art of my cooking again.

I am leaving town. Do not consider me as your legally wedded wife any longer, as I am done with this chapter of my life. Don't waste your time looking for me, you will never find me.

May the whip of the devil punish you and throw your flesh into the depths of Hell.

With pain and tears,
Suria

Tears ran down my cheeks as I read the letter. I concluded that I was in the hands of a monster. I realised that Suria had wanted me to understand that she wasn't a part of Samir's devilish acts. I felt connected to the pain she must have endured and wondered whether she had ever shared her story with anyone before. I found myself worrying about what tactic she might use in order to rid herself of the monster of shame she carried. Would she go as far as to take her own life? If she did, I would probably be the only one who could tell her true story.

After Suria's departure I thought about her as an insect,

one among many trapped in a giant spider's web, which had managed to escape. We were indeed insects trapped in a web.

After a few hours, Samir came into my room and asked me how I was but I didn't answer him. I handed Suria's letter to him, a piece of paper which I was pretty sure would tear him apart. As he read it he tugged at his hair roughly. When he had finished reading, he grabbed me tightly by my head and banged it against the wall. I felt the force of Suria's revenge when Samir began to cry. He yelled at me louder than I had ever heard him yell before.

"Where is she?" he cried out, "Tell me everything you know, Eba!"

"I have no idea!" I told him.

Samir left the room angrily. His footsteps hardened as he made his way down the stairs, shouting to his guards, "Where is my Suria? Why am I paying you fools?"

An image sprang into my mind, of Suria holding hands with a handsome man with a light pencil moustache. A man who didn't use perfume but smelled sweet naturally. I saw him lift her up and kiss her, and her smile. They would go to a place where Suria would have less to worry about, a place where she would be free. They would have children and discover peace. I wished a lot for Suria in my mind, but unfortunately my wishes were not for sale. Had they been for sale, Suria could have bought them all.

After a difficult afternoon, Samir started to calm down a little. A wise man once said to me that through calmness one could find his inner peace. I must have found a moment of inner peace which helped me to unconsciously fall asleep. People say that sleeping in the afternoon is a sign of someone getting older, but in my case it was because I was exhausted.

When I opened my eyes, it was already nightfall. Samir was next to me, lying flat on his stomach sobbing silently, and when he eventually spoke I could hear the bitterness in his voice.

"I did everything I could to make her happy and keep her safe," he said. "I did what a man must do. I provided for her every need and protected her, and now this is what she thinks I deserve. Now my Suria is gone. It is a blessing that I have you, Eba. You are the only one I have now."

He grabbed my body and embraced me, an embrace which became a forceful hug as he started taking advantage of my innocence again. Samir started crying as he pushed himself into my behind. He did it again and again until he was satisfied, then he lit a stick of cigarette and left me alone in my room.

I could have filled a piss pot with my tears. An hour or so later, Samir returned to my room and lay next me on the mattress until we fell asleep. I felt like a man with a shattered dream.

It was about midnight when I heard banging from downstairs. It sounded like gunshots. Samir, as smart as he was, woke up instantly and lifted the mattress which he hid underneath, as flat as a snake. My tension rose when I heard the banging of doors downstairs and the sound of things falling onto the floor. The noise reminded me of when, during the war, the rebels had desperately raided small villages in search of rations.

Suddenly the door of my room was opened and someone appeared with a flashlight pointing straight into my face.

"Where is, Samir?" a male voice demanded roughly, he sounded like an old speaker doing its best to keep the party going.

"I don't know!"

The man stood still for a moment and said to me, "Today is your lucky day. You will survive today not because you are a witness for what is happening here right now, but because you are our messenger." He paused for a moment, his eyes scanning the room, before continuing, "Let me ask you one thing boy. What is your name?"

"My name is Eba," I answered as quickly as possible.

He pointed the automatic rifle he was carrying straight at me.

"Let me tell you one thing, Eba. Here in the abandoned city we value messengers a hundred times more than witnesses. And you happen to be one lucky messenger. When Samir returns home tell him to bring me my money. All of it. Tell him if he fails to do so I will surely visit everyone he loves including his ancestors and in a very robust manner. Do you hear me?"

"I will tell him, sir."

When the armed man turned his back to leave the room I relaxed enough to take a better look at him. He was only a couple of inches short of six foot and was dressed in a black jumpsuit. I sighed with relief and thanked God that I would see another day. I heard the man talking downstairs, which made me certain he was not alone in his mission.

The entire house fell into silence again and Samir lifted

the mattress and looked up cautiously. He was sweating like a lone rice farmer trying to harvest his crop as quickly as possible under the burning dry-season sun before the farmer's crop dries out. I wondered how Samir had managed to survive the heat under the mattress in my poorly ventilated room.

Once the armed men had left the house, I immediately regretted that I hadn't taken my revenge on Samir by turning him in to his angry visitors. My conscience told me I was weak for not doing so after all the dirty things Samir had done to me, but I reminded my conscience that if I had done so they would have probably considered me to be a witness rather than a messenger.

I recalled someone once telling me that every advantage has its own disadvantage, and that sometimes you have to let the porridge get cold before you can taste all the ingredients used to prepare it.

Samir's body gradually emerged from under the mattress, as he crawled out like a snake coming out of hole to warm its skin on a hot day. His eyes expressed intense fear and he spoke hastily.

"We have to leave right away, Eba. Are you sure they have gone?"

I nodded my head like a five-year-old boy. I too was anxious about leaving the slaughterhouse. We left the room quickly but quietly, hurrying down the stairs to the living room.

It was obvious to me that the bodies of the four men I saw lying dead on the floor were Samir's guards. I recognised them from my arrival at the house. As they lay motionless on the floor, at the end of their services to Samir, blood slowly poured out of their brains. I had no doubt that all of them had been shot in the head at close range.

Samir and I left his house like ghosts, or secret agents on an undercover mission. We took our time as we walked carefully but purposefully, as if we were escaping from a maximum security prison. We took cover by leaning on the walls and behind every door along the way. Slowly and quietly we negotiated our way through the back door and then out of the compound by jumping over the concrete fence. Samir stopped a taxi cab which approached ahead of us.

"Do you like reggae music? Do you know who the king of reggae music is?"

The taxi driver fired rapid questions at me as he drove. I could see his two gold front teeth in the rear-view mirror, each designed with the sketch of a pistol at the centre. If I had answered his questions I risked giving him the wrong ones, so I just held my tongue tightly behind my teeth even though I did know who the king of reggae music was. Alimamy's mother had once bought me a black T-shirt with a print of his face on it as a Christmas gift. I thought the taxi driver talked too much, particularly as Samir had asked him to speed up because we were running late for an important meeting.

The heat inside the airless cab was uncomfortable. I found the music disturbing and, again, I had no idea where we were headed. The yellow cab was so old that I could see the ground through a hole in its rusty metal floor. The driver was heavy on the gas, and the speedometer showed he was doing almost a hundred kilometres per hour.

Samir and the taxi driver were speaking in their local dialect with strong regional accents. The two men couldn't hold their tongues and continued chatting until we reached our destination. The car slowed down before the engine died out. We had arrived at a small fishing community.

"Good luck my friend," the taxi driver called to me before he drove off.

There were more than ten small fishing boats grounded on the shore, all of them broken. Two of them were under repair as men were busy hammering and caulking the old timber. Fishing net patching and other domestic activities were going on alongside the carpentry.

The tide was gently coming in and the waves hit the sandy shore at the wharf softly. A group of women sat on the sandy ground, waiting for their beloved fishermen to arrive back from the open sea.

"This way," said Samir in a commanding voice, pointing with his forefinger toward the direction of a lone colourful mansion built on top of a small hill. It was about five hundred meters away from where the main fishing activities were taking place. The shiny house at the top of the hill signified the difference of class in the fishing community, as the houses beneath it were mostly built of clay.

I followed Samir along the beach, like a pet dog on a leash, as we made our way to the hilltop. Samir's heavy breathing as we climbed the hill made me wonder about his physical heath. As we finally arrived at the stairs that led up to the main door of the building Samir monitored my footsteps closely. He acted as if he was a guard watching over a prison-er of war in an escort to a court martial-trial. When I turned around and glanced at him I saw that his face was humourless.

The soothing sound of a violin coming from inside the house brought back sad memories of my late mother and reminded me how much I missed my friends. I started reflecting back to some of the beautiful things I had left behind and wondered whether I would ever see my homeland again. The violin played on as we waited for the door to be opened. The song 'When shall I see my home again' came into my mind and I shed a little tear. That was a song every child born on the soil of my country, the Republic of Yougosoba in the Continent of the Lions, knew well. A song which we sang mostly during times of war.

After the first knock Samir pushed the door which opened easily and we stepped inside. The music stopped for a moment as Samir greeted the violinist in his local dialect, then resumed at a much slower and more romantic pace. We were standing by the door in the living room when the violinist finally turned around. She appeared to be in her mid-thirties and was dressed in a red and black flamenco dress which was bordered with golden frills around the neck. Perfectly fitting her shape, the dress ran neatly over her thighs and all the way down to the floor where it spread into a circle around her. On her head, she wore a little brown comb, shaped like a butterfly, which clipped her hair neatly at the back.

She looked elegant and had wild eyes as she looked at us briefly before taking off majestically on her toes like a cat. She was barefoot and I could see the smoothness of her heels until she disappeared into one of the rooms along the corridor.

After a few minutes, a man with dark curly hair appeared from the room she had gone into and came towards us. The man seemed unhappy as he hugged Samir. I was curious when I saw tears running down the cheeks of the two grown-up men and it made me wonder whether they were shedding crocodile tears or if those tears came from their hearts.

I couldn't contain my emotion and I also shed a few tears. My weakness when I was younger was that when I saw someone crying I would inevitably cry too. As a result I frequently cried for reasons entirely unknown to me.

Samir introduced me to his friend, who quickly escorted us to a room with a big bed and a wardrobe designed with a mirror as one of its doors. There was a transparent glass window overlooking the sea, which was heavily barred.

"You must stay in this room until I tell you to go outside. Meanwhile, I am going to make some arrangements for us to cross over to the Promised Land. Remember, you are all I have now. If you joke with my bread, I will joke with yours too," Samir threatened.

I felt nervous when Samir started undressing, first removing his gown and then a cotton cloth which was tied around his waist. He opened the cloth, which had also served as a waist belt, and started unloading money from it. A variety of foreign currencies emerged, all clean and new. I couldn't begin to imagine why Samir was travelling with such a huge amount of cash.

"I saved this money because I knew days like this would come," he said, "Some people think that money is just material, but to me money is the main cord to human existence. Happiness, livelihood and raising a family are all about money." His voice shook as he spoke and I could see how far he would go to make more money. "We would be stuck here now, somewhere between the desert and the sea, if it wasn't for this money. Do you see that island across the ocean, Eba?" he asked, pointing his index finger toward the window. I could see a little piece of land but it wasn't clear enough to tell how big or small it was.

"That is the Promised Land," he said, "We can pay the fare to cross the sea and get there, but we can only pay in cash Eba, not in good talk or promises."

He packed the money into separate bundles of currency before embracing me forcefully. "I am going to pay for our freedom. You must trust me once more because as soon as we set foot on the soil of the Promised Land we will definitely find the treasure. Our problems will be over then and I will let you go free so you can do whatever you desire. But until we get there you must listen to my advice."

I was watching the sunset from the barred window in our lodging room when I saw a blue car approaching the house. The fishing activities at the wharf were drawing to a close for the day as the fishermen and market women left the wharf to join their families at home. Their departure turned the earlier busy wharf into a quiet leisure beach and stray dogs and cats began to appear on the wharf. The strays set about their routine for daily survival, feasting on the fish waste left behind by the fishermen. Even though there were fights over the bones of contention, the animals ended up settling their differences and sharing the catch.

"Open the gate!" the house boss shouted. The chains securing the front gate were immediately untangled by the gateman and he opened the metal gate widely for the approaching car to enter the compound. The gateman wore a brown uniform with a cap on his head. He had a whistle tied with a knotted string to his breast pocket which made him look like a professional guard. As the car made its way into the compound, the gateman stood still on salute as an honourable welcome to the new arrivals. His gesture reminded me of my first saluting lesson during my preliminary training in the army, when staff sergeant Njai had told me and the other recruits that the salute is the most important sign of respect in the army.

Slowly, the car drove into the compound leaving tyre marks on the soft, sandy soil. Four young girls, accompanied by a lanky but good-looking fellow, looked disoriented as they stepped out of the car.

I wondered whether the young man was playing the same role which Samir had played during our journey across the desert. He looked content as he led the girls toward the stairs at the back door. The girls looked poor and in discomfort as they followed the leader and I watched them until they disappeared out of my line of sight.

Samir was still busy packing away his money, wrapping it into a piece of cloth. When he had finished, he shot me a warning look and left me alone in the room.

A few hours later, the door was opened by one of the security guards, in the same uniform as the one who had opened the gate for the car, and he forcefully pushed the four girls into my room. Aggressively, he closed the door from the outside and I heard the click of the padlock.

The girls, who were around the same age as me, were already sobbing when they entered the room, with tears streaming down their cheeks like an untouched waterway. After a few minutes of crying, they became quiet and their silence lasted for nearly half an hour. I contemplated for a moment, thinking about how I could turn the situation around, as it seemed to me that things were getting out of hand. While I was thinking, one of the girls looked at me and said, "Don't even think about escaping from them, the way back home is already closed."

"What do you mean?" I asked her.

"Two weeks ago a woman who worked here as a servant helped to facilitate my escape, but their network is large and powerful," she said. "After two days of freedom I was found in the desert by two of their patrol men and they turned me over to my owner."

"How did you know I was thinking about escaping?" I asked her.

"I can see it in your eyes. When I look at you I see bravery, ambition and courage."

I heeded the warning in the girl's story and quickly changed my mind about trying to escape. I inhaled deeply and asked one of the girls, "Where did they take you from?"

"We were taken from different places. My name is Jemilla. I was taken from my aunt in the village of Yalu in the south of Cacao."

The three others stopped crying as the discussion between Jemilla and I intensified. One of them joined in and began to tell me her story.

"My name is Massa. I was on the streets in the city of Bong with these two girls selling pure water when a man came to us and asked us to go with him to a feast where people would buy all our pure water. We were excited by his offer and followed him. After walking for about half an hour, we arrived at an isolated road where a red minibus stood. He told us to get into the minibus which we did, and that was where our problems began. There were three other men waiting inside the bus who grabbed us, blindfolded us with white cotton bags and tied our hands behind our backs with a rope. They drove off with us and after several hours of driving we arrived at an abandoned building. Then they removed our blindfolds and promised to take us to a place where we could work and earn more money than selling pure water on the streets for loose change. They told us we would never have to go back on the streets selling water and that we were going to become rich people. Since then, we've been taken to many places where our bodies were touched without our consent by different men. I was a virgin before they abducted me, but my virginity was brutally taken by a big man with a disgusting beard all over his face."

Massa had a fair complexion and a petite, oval-shaped face which made her look simply beautiful. The other two girls, Sallie and M'mama, sat quietly while Massa told their story. In my imagination, I had a vision in which the girls were four innocent lost princesses, longing to go home and wanting nothing more than to see their father the king. When they spoke their voices sounded faraway, as if they were out of reach somewhere in the wilderness. In my vision I saw four princesses tied up together like a bunch of beautiful, freshly-picked red tulip flowers that had been abandoned and left behind by someone who didn't know their worth. In that moment, I almost tore myself up through my own fury. I felt like a beast without claws. Their devasting story made me forget about my own agony. I wished I could get us all out of that place, that miserable golden cage in which we had been locked . But again, my wishes were not for sale, Otherwise, Jemilla, Massa, M'mama and Sallie could have bought them. Jemilla interrupted my thoughts, "The woman who helped me said that I should do everything possible with my mind and strength to escape, because otherwise I would be sold to a wealthy man from an oil-rich continent." "Are we going to be sold too?" asked M'mama.

"Who knows," answered Jemilla. It seemed she had lost the energy even for tears, and was ready to accept whatever fate had in store for her. The other girls, although deeply frightened, had also lost their strength and I could tell that they too had surrendered themselves into a doom world.

It was late at night already and the girls finally fell asleep. I was still awake, looking at their tired and innocent faces. I couldn't sleep. I wished I had the means to transform myself into a hundred strong men and tear our abductors apart to rescue those four innocent souls. I had just dulled the flame of the kerosene lamp when I heard the padlock on the door clinking. The door was opened by a guard who entered our room and walked over to Jemilla. Without speaking, he opened a water bottle and poured cold water onto her face. She woke up instantly, in a state of confusion and clearly disoriented. She stood up, still half in slumber, and looked around the room.

"Follow me!" the guard ordered.

Still dazed, Jemilla couldn't understand what was going on around her and before she could come to her senses the guard started dragging her from the bed. He dragged her forcefully on her back across the bare floorboards into the corridor where she realised what was happening and began to put up some resistance.

The chaos woke the other girls up and they shouted out loudly for help, but their cries couldn't help Jemilla as the guard dragged her away.

We heard Jemilla's screams from the boys' quarters at the back of the house, her dreadful wailing kept us awake. We were terrified about what the guard was doing to Jemilla and there was no chance that we could sleep until her desperate cries stopped. I assumed she was being raped and prayed to God to show us that he really existed by saving her, and us, from this unimaginable horror.

"Maybe someone has bought her already," said Massa, in a cold voice. I looked at her and furiously hissed, "Then that person is a coward."

Samir interrupted our conversation unexpectedly. "What are you two talking about?" he asked as he entered our room silently.

"Nothing," I replied.

He left the room as abruptly as he had arrived and headed back to the living room where he and his friends drank and talked loudly until late into the night.

Across The Ocean

When I woke up in the morning, I was the only one left in the room. I was surprised when I noticed the other three girls were also missing, and assumed they had been taken away while I slept.

I jumped out of the bed and looked through the window at the light-grey cloudy sky. I hoped I would see traces of the taken girls, but to my disappointment there wasn't a single one. I bowed my head down for a moment and then took a second look outside through the window, but there was no one I recognised.

I stood at the window, looking down at the wharf. It was starting to get busy with people arriving steadily as the daily fishing activities began. I started wondering whether the girls were still nearby, and whether they were still alive. I moved nearer to the door for a moment to listen carefully for any sounds coming from inside the house, but the entire house was in silence. It seemed like the alcohol had taken control the previous night and put those savages into a deep sleep. I tried to open the door, but it was locked from outside. I began thinking again about making an escape plan until I remembered the words of warning Jemilla had given me the previous day. But on the other hand, I thought to myself, a man is nothing if he doesn't take calculated risks. My father took the risk of climbing tall palm trees to harvest the

wine from them in order to feed his family, an act he continued doing even after one of his friends had fallen down from
a palm tree one afternoon and died, so it surely made sense
for me to take a chance that may take me out of the hands of
wicked people. I concluded that attempting to escape from
Samir's hands, despite the risks, was the only real option I
had.

When I returned to the window, I saw a boat approaching
from the foggy sea. It was full of people. As the boat came
closer to the shore, I could make out the words 'Living Wood'
painted on its side in green lettering. The boat was made of
wood and painted with sky blue at the top and red at the
bottom, demarcating its Plimsoll line. I heard loud male
voices talking and the sound of babies crying as the crowded boat finally slammed up on the wharf's shore. I was distracted when I heard the padlock on my door rattle. Samir
came into the room and barked at me, "Hurry up, Eba, it is
time for us to leave for the Promised Land." I had no other
choice but to follow my master. Samir and I, accompanied
by two of his friends, left the house and took the steps leading down to the wharf. I kept turning around, checking that
nobody was following us. On one of these turns I caught the
eyes of the violin player from the previous day. She stared
down at us from the top of the stairs where she stood alone.
I smiled at her, and she smiled back as she waved to me with
her right hand.

Getting closer to the boat gave me new a hope, though I
didn't know what was going to happen to us once we reached
the other side of the sea. I told myself that I would have to
trust in what Karamokoh, the traditional healer, had said to
me before I left. He had said that my life would change for

the better as soon as I arrived at the Promised Land and remembering his words replanted a little seed of hope in my mind. The little seed of hope told me that the treasure was there waiting for us. Despite my hope, I knew that I couldn't trust Samir and I longed for the day to come when he would set me free at the Promised Land as he had assured me he would.

"Hurry up, we have limited time before the tide is too high," one amongst the boatmen urged us when we arrived at the shore. He was a strongly built man with long hands. His task was to accompany the people who were coming to join the boat and he lifted me in his hands and threw me into the boat as if I was a small bundle of paper. I landed forcefully in the boat, at the feet of a huge man with a short and stocky neck. The man sat next to a bundle of what looked like his belongings, with his legs outstretched. The boat was already overloaded. As I tried to make myself comfortable, I saw Samir landing in the boat with the same motion as I had just a few seconds earlier. He forced his way aggressively through the heads of the other passengers, squeezing his way passed them towards me.

"Make way you pigs," I heard Samir shout as he made his way through the overcrowded boat. The passengers immediately cooperated with his demand as he pushed through them and I watched as one female passenger hurriedly shifted herself to create some sitting space for Samir, who was clearly determined to sit next to me.

The boat's captain greeted him, "Hello Samir. I got your message. Everything has been arranged."

The captain was a tall man with a slim body and his

weather-beaten face made him look like an old pirate. He had thin lips surrounded by a grey French fork style beard. His mouth twisted as he finished smoking an unfiltered wrap stuffed with local tobacco while he scanned the faces of his passengers.

Samir focused his attentions on observing the activities in the boat, deliberately ignoring the captain's comment. Despite his attempt to pretend he didn't know the captain, I believed that they knew, and understood, each other well.

The boat rocked violently when the waves started to hit its side. The petrol fumes, combined with the heat which came from the choking passengers, upset my stomach and I began to feel seasick even before we had left the shore. It was not a surprise to Samir that I felt sick, he knew that the trip was my first sea adventure.

The sea was cold and the early morning wind increased the strength of the waves as they rolled powerfully toward the shore. As it got colder, Samir opened his bag and took out a warm jacket which he handed over to me.

"Put this on," he said, "it is going to be very cold at the middle of the sea." He took out a dark green bottle with the words 'Dry Gin' written on its yellow label. He gently removed the stopper and drank desperately and greedily from the bottle, until the clear liquid only reached half way up, before replacing the stopper firmly. He clearly had no intention of sharing.

My heartbeat quickened when the captain pulled back the cord, which brought the outboard machine spluttering into life. The boat was still anchored not far from where the daily fishing activities were under way. The captain signalled to his boatmen to draw the anchor on-board and the Living Wood made a dramatic turnaround as it headed out to the foggy sea. The seventy-five horse power outboard machine was screeching, determined to explore the rough waves.

"Listen up everybody!" The captain called us to attention and addressed the passengers on his overcrowded boat.

"My name is Captain Sane. I am the chief captain of this boat. I want you all to know that the line between life and death is a very thin one, like a thread. The thin line now is this boat, the wood that is carrying us. Under my captainship there is no place for panic. This will be the tenth trip I have made to the other side of this sea and each one has been successful. Stay calm and don't move from the positions you are in. I will conclude by wishing you all an enjoyable trip." The way he ended his speech made him sound like he was the captain of an expensive cruise boat, but I was unconvinced. To me, it felt like we were aboard a dangerous death trap.

The first half-hour of the journey passed in silence, except for the voice of a man who preached in the name of God. He prayed, calling for the calms of the sea.

"I pray for calm right now, just like how the Prince of Princes calmed the sea," the preacher proclaimed. Sweat ran down his forehead as he performed his rituals. He preached with his hands opened wide and raised up to the sky. I wondered whether God was present with us at that moment, but I saw only signs of impending disaster hanging in the dark-grey sky. As we proceeded, the fog ahead of the boat became denser and more foreboding. The grey sky turned into different deep colours, first orange then red, before it finally looked a like mass of burning toxic substance. Even though the omen ahead of us wasn't good, the boat maintained a calm and steady course as it pierced its nose through the waves.

A couple of dolphins jumped acrobatically from the water and suspended a few inches in the air before dropping back into the water. It looked like a romantic ritual was taking place inside the water world. I imagined myself in a beautiful garden where, frolicking with someone I truly loved, I threw myself on the floor like the dolphins did in the air. I smiled as I watched the dolphins, they reminded me of the pigeons I used to see, preening each other with love, in the jungle around my village. The scene I had created in my head took me so deep and far that I almost forgot I was in a moving death trap. When I came to my senses, Samir's head was on my right shoulder. His eyes were closed and he was snoring rhythmically. A trail of saliva ran down his chin, which made him look like a sleeping bear in the jungles of Yougosoba at risk of being captured or killed by its human predator.

By the time the dolphins had finished their dramatic display I felt ice-cold. A baby started crying loudly. The baby wailed bitterly as if somebody had pinched it so hard that it had reached the baby's bones, a pain I empathised with. The baby's mother was a young and unhappy looking woman with a distressed frown on her face. I watched as she slipped her hand into her bosom and took out one of her breasts, manoeuvring her nipple gently into the baby's mouth. The comfort of her breast milk helped soothe the crying baby temporarily but the silence didn't last long before the baby started crying again, this time wailing even more intensely. The baby's cries woke Samir and some of the other passengers who had also been sleeping. The atmosphere in the boat had changed from serene to astir. Passengers began talking to each other and their chatting made the boat sound like a small market place with people speaking different languages.

"Pay attention," Samir warned me, "we are now in the middle of the sea."

The wind was gaining strength and speed and it felt, and sounded, quite different than it had an hour earlier. Against the howling wind, the boat continued its robust advance across the wild waves.

"Put on your life jackets and stay calm," the captain announced.

I felt drops landing on my face as it started to rain and watched as the weather changed dramatically. Within minutes we were in a storm which was quickly followed by the strikes of thunder and lightning. There were only a few life jackets in the boat compared to the number of passengers on-board. I was lucky I had one, an orange vest which Samir had given me shortly after we had boarded. People were becoming restless as the storm, and the rain, continued to intensify. After just a few minutes, I was soaked through to my skin and began shivering feverishly, partly due to the cold and partly to my nerves. My jaw stiffened when I tried to speak so I sat in silence, my nose running with crystal-clear drops which tasted salty as they jellied on my upper lip. The wails and screams of the young children on-board were almost drowned out by the shouting of the adult passengers. People started to move around which caused the boat to become unsteady. The waves were getting bigger and the already dark sky was turning even darker. It looked like the night was falling in the middle of the day.

A huge wave slapped the boat violently which caused all of us to panic. We were dislodged from our positions and people fell onto each other. The captain didn't speak but it appeared he had lost command of his boat. I saw him struggling with the handle of the outboard machine, desperately trying to keep the boat steady, but every attempt he made was defeated by the waves.

"No matter what happens just hold on and stick with me," said Samir. He was soaked through and shivering uncontrollably. Samir and I were both speaking with heavy tongues as if we had been poisoned with raw caustic soda. The risk of the boat capsizing was clearly increasing. In my mind, I started saying a prayer to seek my uncle's forgiveness, a moment which set me free and gave me hope. I had a fleeting thought, which brought me some comfort, that if I was going to drown I would leave this world and join my mother in heaven. When I raised my head from my prayers, I saw a giant wave ahead of the boat which the captain tried his utmost to navigate, but the only choice he had was to face it. The giant wave hit the boat ruthlessly and it almost capsized under its force. I heard cracking sounds as the gigantic nails came loose from the grip of the timber the Living Wood was built from. The chaos on-board made it look as if we were witnessing doomsday.

As the frenzy increased, the situation rapidly got out of hand. Suitcases and other personal belongings were floating in the water and being carried away by the rough waves which the boat still struggled to sail through. The crying of young children and women continued, but the outboard machine had stopped crying already. The badly damaged boat was filling up with salt water and it had turned so its nose was pointing in the opposite direction. Within a few moments, the boat started to sink as the waves continued to pound what was left of the wood. Another wave, as high as a mountain, advanced violently towards the boat and, under its threat, some people jumped off the boat before it could sweep them off. I was convinced that we were going down to the drains of the sea. I couldn't even remember my prayers at that point, my concentration had been lost to everything that was happening around me. The giant wave approaching us was my focal point and I took a deep breath as it was about to hit the boat. At the time, I couldn't distinguish the thin line between staying alive and dying. Trying to figure out what to do, I heard a heavy splash of water which sounded like a thunderbolt striking my ear. The giant wave took every person and thing in the boat and swept them away. The cries for help I heard from the drowning passengers were devastating. Samir and I were lying across a floating wooden plank which we gripped on to as tightly as our limbs would allow, both of us unable to speak. It crossed my mind in that moment that he was probably thinking about how to save himself first from the bitterness of death.

I struggled to stay afloat on the plank, but it was too difficult and I lost my grip on it several times. Samir also lost his hold on the plank and I witnessed him struggling in the water trying to avoid drowning.

During the course of Samir's fight to stay alive, I fell into a state of unconsciousness. I could vaguely hear the tweeting sounds of birds flying overhead, but they sounded far away. I didn't know where I was or what was going on around me.

Bodies were floating around in a death pool. With the help of mother luck, I saw an empty five-gallon cooking oil container floating alongside me which I grabbed and hung on to. The idea of hanging on to a container came from a story I'd once heard about some traders who drowned, off the coast of the neighbouring Kikomboso Land, during a trading trip. The story teller had described how one woman had survived that boat accident by hanging on to an empty oil container. That day, my empty yellow container become my life-saving jacket. I was relieved that I had avoided drowning, but I had no idea how long it would take before help would arrive, or whether it even would.

After the devastating storm had passed there was a period of complete and almost surreal calm. My body continued to shiver uncontrollably in the freezing cold sea. I felt a pecking sensation on my feet as living species that inhabited the world under the sea nibbled on my soles. The giant wave that had terrified us moments before became calm, as if it had nothing to do with the disaster which had ruined so many people. The calm after the storm brought the sea to a stable state, though the rain continued and made holes on the surface of the water. The sky, which had been dark like smoke during the disaster, transitioned into a clear blue colour and a faint rainbow appeared in it. My eyes absorbed the image before me while the raindrops sprinkled onto floating dead bodies, bodies of people I saw not too long ago with signs of hope on their desperate faces. The body of one of the babies floated passed me. I noticed the dead body of the preacher who had earlier lifted his hands up high in the sky and asked for the helping hand of God. He floated with his hands on his chest, holding on tightly to his holy book in which the words of his faith were written. The captain, and many others I recognised, floated in the water.

My state of terror rose as more bodies appeared from the depths of the sea, many were clustered together as the waves carried them slowly further out to sea.

As for Samir, I didn't know whether he was dead or alive. He was the only person I actually knew in the boat, but after the massacre I couldn't distinguish his body from those of the storm's many other victims. I was alone, alive and surrounded by horror. Bundles, backpacks and suitcases belonging to passengers had been thrown in different directions and were now mingled amongst the dead bodies.

The mayhem at sea made it impossible to distinguish people's belongings. A Spanish guitar, which I remembered belonged to a musician on-board the Living Wood, floated passed. I didn't know the musician's name but I guessed that, like me, he was trying to make his way to the Promised Land where he believed he would find opportunities to showcase his talents.

The tragedy that I had witnessed kept me awake, but I couldn't hold on indefinitely. I was dizzy and hopeless, and the cold water took the last of my energy as I found myself drifting into sleep.

The thought of sleeping on an empty container in the middle of the sea brought me to a state of alertness and forced me keep my eyes open like a sleeping fish. But it reached a point where I couldn't hold on any longer and I felt as if I was half alive and half dead. After a long struggle, I was finally defeated by the powers of the angel of sleep and I was lost into my dreams.

In my slumber, I heard a female voice calling my name in a whisper which echoed as it faded. It sounded like she was not alone as I heard other murmuring in different voices while her voice kept calling my name. Suddenly I had a feeling of déjà vu. In my memories, I could still remember the picture that emerged after the first whisper. It looked like a singing goddess who, along with her little fairies, had come to embrace a lost soul. Their world was splendid, beautified with a touch of gold so that everything in its surroundings gleamed, including their outfits which were designed in different colours of fluorescent beauty. They lyrically referred to their world as the kingdom of love when they sang as they made way for me to pass through the gate. I couldn't hold back when I saw a clear image of my mother. I was certain that it was her, the woman who brought me into this world. She appeared in a glinting white dress holding a bunch of white roses in her hand.

My mother looked delightful, with a broad smile across her entire face. She embraced me with open arms as she stood in the hallway of a house. In the background the goddess continued to sing.

"Welcome home, Son," my mother said gently.

I smiled back at her as we embraced each other. A child feeling the warmth of his mother's embrace. It was a feeling I had longed for throughout my childhood. I felt safe and relaxed in the hands of my own mother, the woman who brought me into this tragic world. Seeing my mother's image in this other life made me realise that what people had so often told me was really true. I indeed looked much more like my mother than I did my father.

The Promised Land

In between the conversation I had with my mother I faintly heard another voice, this time a strange one. The voice had an exotic tone, and it was unfamiliar to me. It was clear enough that I could recognise it to be a female voice, even though she spoke more from her nose than from her throat. My eyes were still closed and I couldn't tell whether the new voice was a part of the conversation I was having with my mother or not. It seemed that I was in between two different worlds which made me it difficult for me to open my eyes as I struggled to come back from my sleep. In a spiritual way, I fought desperately to break through the thin line between life and death. At the end of the battle, it happened that I won as I chose to stay alive. My victory was confirmed when I realised the voices I'd heard were of living people, and we were in a place where there could be rain, wind, snow and sun.

"You are safe now," she said. Her voice cracked when she spoke but the words were clear and loud enough for me to hear. Those first words that came from her mouth inspired me to open my eyes momentarily, though only half way.

"My name is Doctor Islaker," the voice kindly introduced itself, "I am a medical volunteer and I am here to help you. You are now in safe hands. I have given you a first aid heart reanimation which helped to save your life."

When I opened my eyes wider, I saw a middle-aged woman with a determined expression on her oval face. She worked fiercely to bring me back to a complete human being. I noticed that my stomach had risen more than normal, which was apparently because it was filled with the salt water I'd swallowed.

I shed some tears in response to Doctor Islaker's kindness. After the first aid treatment, she and her team did their best to save my life.

Trying to work out where I was, I turned my neck and looked around. I didn't recognise anyone. There was only a group of medics in white overalls and most of them were wearing masks. I raised my head up higher to look through a small round window near to my bed. I tried to figure out where I was, but it seemed we were surrounded only by water. The ship I found myself on was still anchored at sea. I stared at the calm, blue, water before I lost consciousness again.

The rescue ship was called H.M. Saviour, where I received treatment from three different medical teams during my recovery. There were other patients on-board the ship, but I didn't recognise any of them as being passengers from the Living Wood. I desperately wanted to see at least one familiar face and wished I could have seen one of those helpless breastfeeding mothers with their babies.

"Where is Samir?" I cried out.

The medics struggled to understand what I was saying, as my tongue was still as heavy as lead.

"I don't know who Samir is," one of them replied.

I assumed that Samir had drowned and died in the sea. I had a vague memory of seeing him struggling to stay afloat on the plank, but the plank was slapped by a wave and he lost his grip on it and fell into the sea. I never saw him again.

The next day when I woke up, I realised that I had been in a deep sleep after the treatment. I had no recollection of being changed into new dry clothes. I realised it only when I tried to stretch out my arm and saw that there was a cannula inserted in me with a rubber tube containing a clear fluid coming from a plastic bag on the top of a pole near my bed. Throughout the day medics came in to check on me, a routine which continued as they changed shifts.

In the afternoon of my third day on the ship, a man wearing a long white robe down to his feet, with a black briefcase in his hand, came in. He looked straight at me as he appeared from the main hallway.

"Good afternoon. How are you feeling now?" he greeted me as he came to my bed. He introduced himself to me as Joseph Langley and told me that he worked in the border control department of the Promised Land.

I introduced myself too, but only by my first name.

Langley was lanky, but he was neatly dressed and a good-looking young guy. He rolled his fingers through his hair and opened his briefcase. Taking out an official looking blank form he wasted no time in asking me questions regarding my personal information. As well as my name he wanted to know my date and place of birth and details about my father, mother, siblings, wife and any children I had. That was the first time in my life that someone had fired questions at me so rapidly. Langley repeatedly asked me my name, even though I had already introduced myself to him. His repetitive questioning made me tired and I decided not to answer any more of his questions. I expected Langley to understand that I must be exhausted after what I had been through and needed more time to recover, but when I failed to answer his questions he looked at me sternly and said, "You better cooperate with me now, Mr Yoko, these are questions you will have to find answers to anyway."

In my head I said the words 'no comment' to myself.

Langley, who looked determined like a young career lawyer with high ambitions and looking forward to executing his first duty, ignored my silent protest and started to pack his papers away, laying them carefully into his black leather briefcase before he turned around and walked away. The clicking sound made by his tainted brown leather shoes as he proceeded to the main exit grated on my ears. After he'd gone I had the feeling that one day soon he would come back.

The rescue ship's horn sounded as it sailed in to dock at the main port of the Promised Land. The proud medical volunteers standing on the upper deck waved enthusiastically to the workers standing on the dock. I went back to my cabin to prepare for our disembarkation. I sat on my bed wondering where we were and what this place was going to look like to my newcomer's eyes. I had heard a lot about this place and I felt excited to be landing on the soil of the Promised Land.

I had already been informed, by one of the ship's medics, that on our arrival at the mainland I would have to undergo what he described as a background check. This would entail an interview based on which a decision would be made as to whether or not they would officially allow me to stay there. He told me that if the decision was not in my favour, I would be thrown outside of the walls which surrounded and protected the Promised Land.

I still had no idea what had happened to Samir. I hadn't heard anything more about him since that tragic event. On the other hand, it didn't matter any longer as I firmly believed that the scary serpent who used to appear in my worst nightmares had drowned into the belly of the sea. My belief that Samir had died in the accident brought me a huge sense of relief. The master who had bought me and become my legitimate owner. The master who was probably about to sell me on, somewhere in an unknown country. In these moments I had an almost overwhelming feeling of relief. At other times I felt engulfed with pity as images of those innocent crying children flashed through my head.

I later considered that what had happened between me and Samir was similar to the myth of the great Pharaoh and Moses. According to the narrative of what happened to Moses and his people, that saga was another tragic one. I thought that if my story were to be told by someone else one day the story teller would describe me as the Moses of modern times, and Samir as the Pharaoh who perished in the sea. I found myself desperately wishing that I could have done something to save at least some of the lives of those who had died, and felt a deep sadness, and guilt, that I hadn't had the power to do what Moses had done when he commanded the sea to become calm and made a safe passage for his people.

When the H.M. Saviour anchored at the mainland port, one of the medical volunteers came into my room and asked me to clear away my bedding as it was time for me to go. She took a deep sigh and wished me good luck.

I was fit enough to get up and move on to the next stage in my miserable life. "Welcome to the Promised Land," a woman announced.

The woman who welcomed us was short and thin. She was one of a group of three nuns who stood next to a booth on the dockside which was full of essential commodities.

The nuns looked enthusiastic as they welcomed us, the survivors, into a new world. They were wearing black dresses and their hair was covered with black veils, lined with a thin white cloth at the front. Their faces were visible and they welcomed us with warm smiles.

I was in a group comprising nine people who had also been onboard the Saviour. One of the volunteers on-board had already informed me that the people in my group had also been rescued from accidents at sea. The nuns offered us clean drinking water in plastic bottles, along with milk and bread, as we passed through their charity booth of goodwill on our arrival. I was overwhelmed by the nuns' extraordinary kindness and found myself wishing that the world could have more people like them in it.

We were accompanied into a tunnel by a team of four men who looked fit in their blue T-shirts and faded blue jeans. Their outfits gave me the impression they were some kind of national guards.

"All of you this way," the fittest guard amongst them said to us in a sarcastic tone.

The men in uniform looked severe and talked only when they gave us instructions. In a watertight escort, with two men leading the way in front of us and the other two behind us, they led us to the control centre which was in a building close to the port.

We finally arrived at a huge single-storey building, constructed from old brown clay bricks which made it look like an ancient prison. I was surprised to discover that the inside of the building was impressive, boasting a smartly decorated and modern interior. Around the room I noticed a variety of sophisticated electronic devices. The technology employed in the control centre enabled everything that was happening in the locality to be seen and monitored by robots and computers. An alarming thought occurred to me that there could come a time when human beings would only sit down and drink coffee while computers and other machines did the work. The source of my concern had been when I had to use the toilet and asked a guard to show me the way. I was amazed when he referred me to a robot who successfully accompanied me to the toilet, waited at the door until I had finished doing my business and then guided me back to my sitting place. It then thanked me and walked back to its previous post. I was in awe of the robot. If this was truly the modern civilisation people talked about, then I had been hiding like a rat inside a hole all my life.

In the main hall we were made to sit separately, each of us were offered a chair sited a distance from the others, to discourage us from communicating. I sat quietly on my chair, patiently waiting for my interview. The guards who had accompanied us into the building stood at their guard posts with their hands folded across their chests, exuding confidence. The year we arrived at the Promised Land, they were under a high national security alert due to the ongoing unrest in many parts its neighbouring countries. As a result, the newcomers to its shores were thoroughly scrutinized with a system that was trusted by most of its citizens.

After hours of sitting and waiting, instructions were finally announced through the speakers installed on the sparkling white ceiling. I tried to figure out where the voices we heard through the speakers came from.

"Here is a cup of coffee for you, sir." Her voice came

through the speakers attached to her chest and her eyes blinked when she looked at me. I sat up straight in my seat and found myself looking at a one-foot tall robot carrying a serving tray with a cup of coffee in a plastic cup, which she kindly offered to me.

"Thank you but I am fine, I don't need coffee" I said.

The display of robots in the main hall of the control centre was impressive, although I thought it was also dangerous to be served by a machine. I had lived a natural life and was used to working with human beings and sometimes animals, but never with machines. I was used to doing everything for myself and such self-sufficiency brought me a feeling of safety. But I had also been failed many times by my fellow human beings and therefore had to question myself as to why I would so readily dismiss the robot which had kindly served me and showed me the way to the toilet earlier. Drinking a cup of coffee wasn't a high priority for me at that moment, and I was more concerned with the smell that evaporated out of me. I hadn't washed myself properly in the last three days and having a warm shower and a decent meal were my only immediate needs. If it hadn't been for the kindness of those nuns when we arrived, who had given me a carton of milk and two slices of bread, I don't think I could've carried on that afternoon as there was no food at the control centre. I learned later that the milk the nuns had given to us was a product which was served to convicted prisoners for breakfast, and that some prisoners even rejected the milk, preferring to go without food all day rather than consume milk which many people believed was contaminated due to the breeding process of cows in the Promised Land. But I was happy to drink it, and for the first time I gulped down a whole carton of milk without sharing.

"Eba Yoko!" My name was announced through the speakers in a heavy accent which changed its pronunciation.

A guard appeared in front of me and said, "Follow me this way, sir."

I stood up from my seat and followed the guard through three different locked doors which the guard used an electronic pass to open. I hadn't witnessed a process like that before and I wondered how a door could be opened by the swipe of a pass.

The third door took us into the room where I would be interviewed. It was furnished with a metal desk and two single chairs of the same design. On top of the desk stood a computer screen displaying symbols of smiles which changed frequently to show the word 'welcome'.

"You may have a seat," the guard said, "I will stand beside you when your interview commences."

I did as the guard had instructed me, though my abdomen felt as if it was boiling. My stomach twisted violently inside, a symptom of my nerves about the impending interview.

"Hello and welcome to my office. My name is Marina thirty-three," a female voice coming from the computer in the interview room introduced herself before she continued in a sombre tone. "I am going to make an oath before we begin. I, Marina thirty-three, solemnly swear in the name of the King of the Promised Land and its citizens, that I will serve the purpose which I, Marina thirty-three, was commissioned to fulfil. I will do so with respect for the laws which govern this land. Long live the King." Marina paused for a few seconds. "In that respect, sir, I am going to conduct an interview with you regarding your personal circumstances, after which I will carry out a background check. During the check, I will process your details and make a decision. My decision will determine whether or not you are eligible to stay inside the walls of this land. If your background check has no substance according to the law, I am afraid you will be kicked out of the system and thrown out of the walls."

My interaction with the computer astonished me, and I struggled to comprehend how an interview could be conducted by a machine. Before I could settle down she began questioning me.

"What is your name, sir?"

"Eba Yoko," I answered reluctantly as I frowned at the computer as if I was dealing with a human being who might understand my emotional state. I was already feeling frustrated by the authorities in the Promised Land who repeatedly asked me to confirm my name, and this time I was particularly vexed by Marina's request given that she was the one who had called out my name on the speakers in the main hall.

"Tell me what happened to you, Mr Eba Yoko," she asked, finally using my name.

I broke down in tears as I told her my story, though I knew that a computer could not comfort someone in a state of complete despondency or give a pocket tissue to a victim to wipe away tears. A computer could sense and detect things, but it couldn't detect the inner feelings of a human being.

"I'm sorry, Mr Yoko," said Marina. I was surprised by her response, and assumed she had somehow detected my soft sobbing voice, processed it in her system and concluded that I was becoming emotional.

"I understand you are in a state of melancholy, Mr Yoko," Marina said, "Is there anything I could do for you?"

"No, thank you," I said.

"Django, bring Mr Yoko a glass of water please," Marina ordered.

Within a few seconds another robot came into the room, carrying a glass full of cold water. The robot walked over to me unsteadily. I took the glass from the tray and drank it hastily. I thanked Django before it left the room. I looked at the computer again, this time with a sense of compassion, as she sat alone on the desk. But I was worried about seeing a world which was once ruled and dominated by humans transitioning into a world be ruled and dominated by working machines.

When I had finished telling my story, Marina thirty-three asked me to leave the interview room. She told me I would be called back in within an hour to be informed of the outcome of the interview.

I left Marina's office escorted by the same guard who had accompanied me there and we went to another room to wait.

"Eba Yoko, please report to Marina thirty-three," said a voice from the speakers.

I was escorted again by the same guard to Marina's desk. The word 'decision' was displayed on the computer screen. I straightened up and focused my ears attentively on the computer, a machine which was about to decide my fate.

"Due to certain findings which are contrary to the laws of this land, and after several searches, our system has decided that your story is not convincing and lacks proof to support it. Therefore, the system has declared you to be an illegal alien who has broken the rules that govern our borders. As a result, you have twenty-eight days to leave the borders of this land." She lapsed into silence, as I did, before continuing. "You have a right to an attorney who could help you to appeal against our decision, assuming that you can afford to hire one. I wish you good luck."

That was how I was kicked out of the system, by a statement from a little machine standing on a desktop. I was bewildered by the decision because it was totally unexpected. I was under the impression that, since I reached the Promised Land, everything would be all right. I believed that if Marina thirty-three had been human she might have been sympathetic and understood my pain and misfortunes. But she wasn't, and she couldn't override the system.

I was taken away by two guards who accompanied me to a parking lot where a prison bus was waiting. They pushed me, with my hands cuffed behind my back, into the bus, which they referred to as the 'meat wagon'. Inside I joined two men who had also been grilled, and rejected, by the system. The prison bus was assigned to transport illegal aliens to locations unknown to them with maximum security. Armed guards transferring prisoners in chains. When we arrived at our next destination, the door of the bus was opened and a stocky man of medium height appeared and released my hands from the cuffs. His posture reminded me of an image I had once seen of an ancient elf. He wore a strange armband, made of leather, which almost reached his elbow.

"Welcome to the Dune," he said, "here you are free, but your chances of survival will depend on how highly skilled you are. Life is becoming tougher for you dude, there are no sanctuaries here for people like you anymore." He then released me, pushing me through the door which he closed behind me, before the bus drove off with the other passengers still inside. And there I stood, alone in the wilderness. I inhaled a handful of red dust kicked up like a tornado by the giant tyres of the 'meat wagon' as it sped off on the gravel stones of the unpaved road.

I found my way to the Dune, a city inhabited by dilapidated and abandoned buildings. I came across a group of desperate stray dogs searching for anything they could find to eat among the piles of garbage in the streets. The dogs fought each other viciously for the leftovers of a hamburger.

When I began to explore the streets of the Dune, I realised life there was not a level playing field. Prostitution was rife and the misuse of drugs and alcohol the daily norm for the people who dwelled there. I saw people like me, carrying the label of illegal alien. Witnessing those labelled people living in deplorable conditions broke my heart, but at the same time it also gave me some hope because, at least for now, they were still alive. Illegal aliens and even homeless citizens could be thrown outside the walls where they would face the hard side of life and perish. It was heart-breaking to see human beings being rejected by other humans, albeit through the technology of the computer, in the country where they were all born. Boundaries were set and walls were built, according to the rules. The rules that separated the baseborn from the upper crust.

The Dune was painted with the colours of desolation and disappointment.

I had been thrown into the city without any idea that it was going to become my new home. I didn't know a single person there, or where to ask for help, and I doubted whether I could survive in such a place. But I knew that if I wanted to survive I needed to keep myself physically and mentally stable. I lifted my hands and asked the universe for guidance.

A Lesson To Learn

Later that day, I retraced the route I had followed earlier. As a boy who was born along the river, I have always had a special bond with places that have a river or are close to the sea. I also kept in mind what a wise man had once said to me, that the stranger who asks will never get lost. When the wise man's words popped into my mind I used them wisely by asking an old citizen, who had lived most of his life in the Dune, a few questions to get some useful information about the surroundings. That night I had the answers to the things I needed to know as a newcomer. After talking to the old citizen, I took a walk to the rainbow area of the Dune where I met, and spoke to, a twelve-year-old boy. The boy was standing at the street corner selling his body by giving pleasure to its seekers in return for money. I stole a bit of his time and was able to gather some information such as where I could get a free hot meal each day, how I could find medical assistance and where the boulevard along the beach could be found. That night, I had no choice but to pass the cold night on the stairs of a broken and abandoned house which the boy had directed me to and told me I could sleep in. The next morning, I decided to go for a walk along the seaside. It wasn't difficult to find, I followed the road as described to me by the boy I had met the previous night.

After a short walk, I arrived at the seaside where the tide was low and the sun was still on the rise. The yellow light from the sunrise reflected on the sandy beach which made it look like pure gold. The Blue Arrow Boulevard was named by its ancestors in honour and glory of their victory over their colonial masters in the war of their independence one hundred and fifty years earlier. The building of that military garrison still stood at the time I arrived there. Even in present days, the boulevard still remained an important position for the defence of the Promised Land, even though it was abandoned because it was situated in the Dune area. For many people, the area served as a place of rest and meditation.

During my stroll along the boulevard, I saw a man lying on a flat monumental stone. The man looked like one of my countrymen. As I got closer, I saw that he did indeed resemble a true son of the Continent of the Lions. As any other wise traveller would have done, I halted and tried to attract his attention. I waited for the right moment before posing a question, but his focus was completely on the infinity of the sea and his eyes were steady and constantly open. I used another method as I stood close to him, trying to gain his attention. I cleared my throat, expecting him to stand up, but my throat clearing wasn't sufficient to alert his attention which irritated me. I took a bold initiative and tapped him on his shoulder. He slowly raised his head, in a motion like a dinosaur, and finally rested his gaze and focus on me, his big green eyes widening. I was worried, because at that moment I couldn't be sure what his next move would be.

"My name is, Eba," I said, unconsciously speaking in our local dialect. I didn't know what had prompted me to introduce myself first, or why I had done so in a local Yougosoban dialect.

He told me his name was Yalla Banke and gave me a firm handshake, squeezing my fingers hard as his broad palm wrapped around mine.

"Welcome here to the Dune," he greeted me.

Yalla was a bit taller than me and was more strongly built. When I looked at him, I detected bitterness and grief through the expression on his face. The oval shape of his face looked similar to the blacksmith in my village, long and promising. Yalla appeared to be in his early sixties, but in our open discussion, as we shared more details about ourselves, he claimed he was twenty-five, a claim which caused me to raise an eyebrow disbelievingly.

"But you look like sixty," I muttered hesitantly.

"I am twenty-five years old," he said, "I said that because this is my twenty-fifth year outside the walls." He cleared his throat and spat out thick saliva on the floor.

"Several times I've tried to legally break through into those walls, but the computer keeps rejecting me. The consistent rejections have left me empty inside and with nothing but a ruined life. I am forbidden to legally find a job, which has left me jobless for all those years. When I came here, I was a young man just like you. A young man thirsty for knowledge. But it was as if they were the villain who knew what my dreams were and wanted to ruin them, a plan which they executed successfully by rejecting every new application I made.

They denied all my basic human rights. No access to enrol into the educational system. You couldn't believe it, Eba," he said.

"I am not officially allowed to see a medical practitioner even when I am sick. In all those years I haven't once slept with a proper roof over my head. This place is a dumping hole. That is why people call it the jungle." He covered his face with his broad palms, as if he felt ashamed of himself, and wiped tears away with his fingers from the corners of his eyes.

"But there is no jungle here," I interrupted.

"This is a jungle," he continued, "when I first arrived I had the same eyes as you, I could see but I was blind. I survived with a lame optimism, day by day, year by year as time passed by. Now look at me, look how weak and tired I am. I ended up a hopeless fag roaming around a lost city without a future. I have nothing meaningful to offer, not to myself or anyone else. I am just sitting here on my stupid butt, watching the sun rise and set, which looks beautiful but is a waste of time. Twenty-five years!" Yalla cried out loudly as unstoppable tears ran down his cheeks.

On hearing Yalla's frustrations I found myself drowning with him in his emotions. It seemed we were wearing the same shoes, albeit perhaps of a different size or colour.

I began asking myself how I could build a life here in a place which had brought someone like Yalla all the way down to the drains of life. What if I decided to return back home without a piece of the Hundred Golden Horses, a treasure which I had vowed to pay half of its value to Karamokoh Dambay? On the other hand, I didn't have the resources to build a raft which I could row across the ocean and find my way home. After Yalla's dramatic story, I decided I only had one choice, which was to return back home by the route I had travelled to reach the Promised Land. But the sea was dangerous, I had already almost lost my life by drowning. I considered the various obstacles I would be likely to come across on the way if I decided to go back. I asked myself whether I had the courage to make that journey through the deadly scorpions in the wilderness, and how I would find my way in the open and isolated desert, alone in an environment in which I would be completely disoriented.

Such questions triggered fear in my mind at a crucial moment in my life. After being thrown out of the walls of the Promised Land, I had nothing more to hold on to than a branch of disappointment. The Promised Land was where I had expected the best events in my life to occur. It was generally believed and accepted by people on the other side of the sea that reaching the Promised Land was the solution to all a person's problems.

"As soon as you land your feet on the shores of the Promised Land, your problems are over," they would say. It sounded easy, like eating a ripe banana.

At sunset, I picked up my backpack and slung it over my shoulder like a portable closet. It contained all my essential belongings which were given to me on the ship, comprising items such as clothes, toiletries, a shaving machine and foodstuffs. I took a brief look at Yalla and left him sitting motionless on the stone, watching the sunset.

I had to double my steps so that I arrived in time to secure a spot in the long queue of homeless people hoping to get a mattress in the only night shelter.

I was fortunate to have met Yalla. If he hadn't directed me to the night shelter, I would still have been sleeping under the stairs of the dilapidated house the prostitute boy had taken me to, where I had been even more exposed, lonely and vulnerable. Yalla warned me to stay away from frustrated sleepers who are always looking for trouble, especially with newcomers.

The shelter was a vast and partly burned building built with common clay bricks that make it look from the outside like an ancient oven. It had been named the Chocolate Factory before it was bombarded during the invasion of the Grey Aliens during the early days of the war.

The abandoned chocolate factory was used by a charity organisation called 'Frailty for Strength'. Their goal was to provide help to rejected and lost souls of the Promised Land. Their slogan was displayed boldly on the top of the building and as I read it, 'Rebuilding Broken Lives', I wondered whether my new life was a broken one. It was clear that there were some broken lives they could help to rebuild as, in the queue outside, I could see drug addicts and alcoholics as well as people in need of help with other problems. Problems like mine.

That evening, I made my way into the night sanctuary for the first time. Some parts of the original interior were still intact and I could see several of its old installations, production machines and other hardware which were wrecked, stained and rusty. The old machines, hanging from a metal bar across the ceiling right above where I lay my head, appeared life threatening to those of us sleeping underneath them. Single mattresses in rows on the floor of the hall were lined up neatly like an ex-military graveyard. The earlier you made it into the shelter, the better chance you had of securing a mattress. Latecomers had to use old cartons as bedding. There were not enough sleeping blankets for the

people in the shelter which led to wrangling over owner-
ship. I watched and observed, following Yalla's advice to reserve more and give less.

"Let us say a prayer before we take our places," said an
old woman, who I later learned was called Willie and was
the regular guide sleeper who had dedicated twenty years
of her life serving as a volunteer in the organisation. Willie
was a passionate human being who gave all that she could
to make others happy.

"That is my life sentence," she would often say.

In addition to Willie, there were also several other volunteers who came to watch over us at night. They came on different nights and were quite different characters. Some of
them were genuine in the cause of helping people in need,
some were there to exercise their power over the weak and
poor.

One night, a man who walked with crutches because one
of his legs was cut off by a local militia group during a violent period in his country was approached by a mean sleeping assistant who most of us disliked. The sleeping assistant
asked the one-legged man to leave the night shelter because
he had farted, an act which he described as unruly miscon-
duct. The one-legged man refused to leave the shelter and
the two men had a verbal clash, exchanging immoral words.
The following night, the same mean assistant came in accompanied by a huge man who looked like he worked for the
Neighbourhood Watch, the department which was responsible for law and order among illegal aliens in the Dune. It
was midnight and we were already in deep sleep. The shelter was quiet when Mr Stein, the mean sleeping assistant
who according to his claims was an ex-military policeman

during his early life, woke the one-legged man and asked him to go outside. A request which the one legged-man had no other choice but to refuse. He did so, despite the presence of the huge Neighbourhood Watch man whose job was almost certainly to apply force if the one legged-man resisted.

"Grab him and throw him out," ordered Mr Stein. His expression was aggressive and he seemed determined to pick a fight.

The resistance put up by the one-legged man provoked the situation further and he ended up wrestling, a wrestle which didn't last long, with the physically fit Neighbourhood Watch man, grabbed the one-legged man and threw him out of the door like an empty sack. The struggled one-legged landed out of the door closely followed by his crutches, which were thrown on top of him by Mr Stein.

After that event, I suffered many sleepless nights playing it over in my mind, trying to figure out why a disabled man would be thrown out into a dark and cold night for doing nothing more than farting. I also held my backside tight, because I couldn't afford to undergo what the one-legged man had suffered.

A year after my arrival in the Promised Land, I was still in disarray and deeply regretting that I had found myself there. It seemed as if my whole life was flattened by invisible bad spirits.

I looked forward to having some peaceful rest at the night shelter after rough days, but it turned out to be a place where I became afraid. I woke up most nights and sat up straight on my mattress, looking up to the ceiling, because I was terrified that one of those heavy metal machines hanging above my head would fall on me during my sleep. Willie, who I later learned was seventy years old, was the only one who used to wake me up from my nightmares. She understood the problems of lost people, and their sleepless nights and nightmares. Willie herself was once a lost soul. She told me one night about how she had slept rough on the streets when she was thrown out of the walls by her own people.

"While I have described it that way, I have to confess it was all my fault."

"I was born and raised with all opportunities as a citizen of the land, but I blew all my chances by choosing the wrong side of the coin."

She explained to me how she became a drug addict at the age of seventeen when she ran away from her parent's home through the influence of bad friends.

"But I only regret the things that I never tried to do. The pain which I am going through right now makes me feel strong and alive." Her words were inspiring to me, as I was a young man who must grow and learn a lot as far as life was concerned, and I was ready to learn through listening to experienced people like Willie.

"No matter where life takes you Eba, you will have a great future" she assured me one quiet night.

Like Willie's vision about my future, I believed there were many others illegal aliens who also had promising futures. A man had once said to me, when we had just arrived at the night shelter, "It doesn't matter whether you pass the night in a five-star hotel or under a tree. When the sun rises in the morning, everyone will have the same feeling about another night in this life and would say 'Yes, I have passed the night' the same as everybody else." The man looked proud when he spoke and, although his narrative might not be the reality for everybody, it sounded hopeful. I felt hope by my side every morning when I woke up, and was always thankful that I had lived to see another sunrise.

There were rumours going around the shelter that a formidable group of financial donors provided the money to run the organisation that sheltered us. I was curious as I had never set eyes on the foundation's donors. I wasn't sure whether that really mattered, but I did wonder if some day those rich people would come in person and spend some time with us. A move which, in my opinion, might help us to have a sense of belonging and could make us feel like human beings. But in the Promised Land, due to the state in which I found myself, the most important thing was to have a slice of bread with peanut butter at the shelter each morning. It was a bite which was significant because it helped me stave off the devastation of hunger for most of the day. For dinner, there was also an option to join the long line at the Holy Sisters' Charity, an organisation which saved the lives of many. All except the latecomers.

Those days of my life were not easy. The ration routines were different than they had been at my grandmother's kitchen while I was still a little boy. My grandmother's kitchen was a place I could walk into majestically, even in the middle of the night it didn't matter, I just knew to be quiet as I helped myself to a full plate of rice and beans. But here in the Promised Land, I learned a lot about the importance of being on time, like 'sharp is sharp', especially when it came to charitable events. Otherwise 'late is late' and the door would be closed.

In my village time worked with the seasons, which was why most people slept in until the sun came up. The idea of the twenty-four seven economy is not something our great-grandfathers thought of, and such a motivation was not inherited, not even by my father's generation. Even the way people walked there was very slow and relaxed, as if they had no worries at all in the world, compared to the Promised Land where, with its twenty-four seven economy, people always walked in a hurry as if they were worried about being late.

There was a shoemaker in Looking Town who used to say, "When you travel in a hurry, you will arrive late." During my boyhood, his words inspired me to do things like fetching drinking water from the river as slowly as I could, much to the annoyance of my Aunty Agnes. But later on, when I began to reflect back on my lazy behaviour, I remembered that the shoemaker himself delivered a poor quality of service due to his slowness, which created problems for him at the end of the year. He would end up with debt collectors knocking at his door in the early hours of the morning. My uncle used to call him a lazy man too, and he sometimes said, "There is no food for a lazy man."

Even though I had been raised in such an environment, when I was in the Dune I did my utmost to make sure that I was always on time so that I could have a pass into the sisters' kitchen. Missing that daily hot meal would be a misery as it was my only proper meal, and there was no cash in the bag which I could use to buy food at one of the unhealthy fast-food caravans in the Dune.

There were no showers at the night shelter, only a single

broken toilet which was always occupied at any time I attempted to go and relieve myself. Some people didn't even flush their waste, even though there was always a bucket of water available for that purpose. The ugly voice of Mr Stein would wake us up at six-thirty every morning, when most of us were trying to recover from our sleepless night. He would urge us to wake up and be ready to leave the building within an hour. I didn't know what the other sleepers thought about being woken up so early in the morning, and in such a rough manner, but to me it felt like serving a civilised imprisonment.

The one thing that annoyed me the most about being woken up so early in the morning is that there was then nothing for me to do to fill the rest of the day. I had no other choice at the time but to roam around the streets of the Dune, unemployed and doing nothing that could make a difference to my life or to society.

The streets of the Dune were like a disorganised bazaar, shattered and ungoverned. Finding the means to survive was as likely as winning the lottery, especially for someone in destitution. There were days when I couldn't make even a single dime with which I could have at least bought a glass of wine. People had to make tough choices to earn their daily bread. Some illegal aliens choose to cooperate with criminal gangs who worked within the walls. They got involved with the trafficking of hard drugs and other substances. Such activities had ruined the lives of many of the illegal aliens and forgotten citizens of the Promised Land. Most young men and women had no choice but to hang out on the streets and sell their bodies to their secret masters.

The heads of those cartels had a strong syndicate and great skills which they used to motivate vulnerable boys and girls on the street. They would say to them, "It is only a matter of survival. The game of life is like the 'one man's bread is another man's poison' theory. The death of one is the bread of the other." Those who couldn't bear the pressure of spending their lives as drug dealers often became the addicted victims, the fish inside the aquarium. Hopelessness and insolvency had left many in a devastating condition on the streets, which fuelled an increase in crime and violence and exacerbated the tensions between the men in blue and the rejected society. A civilised war which left dead bodies on the street corners every morning.

When I walked on the streets, I always had to turn around and look behind me. My whole body would be overcome by fear and I was terrified that the men in blue would pick me up one day and throw me back into the sea where I almost lost my life. I was always in a state of anxiety which made it clear that I couldn't make a life here in the Dune.

The sun was changing into a vibrant orange colour as it slowly set behind the surface of the sea. It was a beautiful day for November, especially in a country where the snow falls. After being tempted by the beauty of the sunny weather, I had decided to take a walk to the Blue Arrow Boulevard along the beachside, where I thought I may find my friend, Yalla. I wanted to meet him again so we could pick some bones out of the fleshy fish and also enjoy some food for thought with my old friend, as it had been a little while since I had last seen him.

The one-way street leading to the boulevard was busy with

cars and pedestrians of the working classes who lived inside the walls. When I arrived at the seaside, there was a large crowd of people, well-dressed and parading in their expensive cars. Most of them played loud music from their sound systems. I didn't mind that people from within the walls occasionally brought some life into the Dune, although many of their activities appeared staged to demonstrate that they were making a living inside the walls. But the judgemental weigh and measure attitude, which determined how and where people should live, was a sore which hurt many citizens and even made them jealous of the working classes who paid their taxes. This was especially true of those citizens who had misused the opportunities given to them by birth right, and who blamed their suffering on others after losing everything and being thrown out of the walls.

As I strolled along the boulevard, enjoying the atmosphere, I noticed a forming crowd of people who came from all over the land each year to celebrate the liberation of independence. I was told that the Blue Arrow Boulevard was a strategic point, where the then Admiral Simon Speers of the Promised Land's Blue Guard and his men had fought the last battle at sea during the final struggle for independence. At one time the Dune had been a strategic city, but it later became an isolated monument, abandoned and left in the hands of the criminals even though it still belonged to the kingdom.

I didn't dare to walk close to the jubilant crowd whom I considered as superior human beings to me, a man who had been degraded to a homeless vagabond with a number instead of a name. Even though I was born on the doorstep of destitution and raised in a hostile environment, I realised that you can only feel at home when you are home. While I was in the Promised Land, I felt like I was not a man born of a woman and I sometimes wondered whether it was true that I was an alien, a title I first learned from a computer screen.

After a long stroll I found Yalla at his usual spot, smoking a wrap of green weed.

"Do you see this weed I am smoking right now, Eba?" he said, "It comes from the plant of wisdom which many people believe can cure sickness. It also gives peace within when you smoke it."

Yalla's lips were almost burned as he smoked the joint right down to the end.

"The last bit of the smoke gives the most pleasure," he said with a grin.

"Perhaps, if smoking is your pleasure," I replied politely.

Yalla looked rough and tougher than usual after finishing his smoke. The way he spoke made him sound like a wise old man. He smiled as he threw what remained of his joint onto the sand, stamping his foot on it to put it out, and pointed to the sea.

"You see that sun going down right now? It brings me hope. That sunset you are looking at is the only truth I can guarantee. Beyond all doubt, I believe that the sun will come up tomorrow morning even if it doesn't shine." He stopped talking and looked at me straight in the eye and continued, "I have given my heart to many people before, Eba, but the outcome has always been disappointing."

"What do you mean?" I asked inquisitively.

"I trusted a thousand times, and a thousand times my heart was left broken." His shoulders slumped, as if to express his disappointment. "That is why I surrendered all my trust to that sun we're watching and believe that it will surely come up again tomorrow." He bowed his head to his chest, the gesture of someone who has been let down.

For me the issue of trust was still a complicated one. I wondered why I would stop trusting people when I needed help, especially in a land where I couldn't do much to help myself and didn't knowing many people. After giving it some thought I decided that Yalla's philosophic explanation about the issue of trust had a personal reason.

Yalla turned to me and said, "Eba, I would like to introduce you to a friend of mine who is a citizen living inside the walls and is well connected to the authorities there. You are a young and healthy man, which gives you a chance to build a life here even though you've been declared an illegal alien."

Yalla's suggestion sounded promising. Somewhere in the back of my mind I questioned whether I should trust him to introduce me to his friend, a person I didn't know, given what had happened at Samir's house and in other places. A damage which had become a decay I could barely fix. But on the other hand, it didn't seem wise to dump the feet of a new friend into dirty shoes. How could I judge the friend of Yalla if I didn't agree to meet him?

I mulled over the issue in my mind and concluded that Yalla's friend might be a good person.

"I would like to meet your friend," I said in a small, hesitant voice.

"You never know what the rain might bring you, Eba. Normally I don't bring new people to my good friends. As you know, many other people in your situation are looking to meet such a person, someone who will bail them out of this pit which we all have fallen into."

I thanked him respectfully for his kindness.

"Don't even mention it," said Yalla. "From the first moment you approached me I knew there was a divine connection between us."

His final words convinced me that Yalla Banke was a good person. Those were sentiments no one had ever expressed to me before.

At nine the following morning, as we had agreed, Yalla and I met at a park close to the night shelter. It was raining as I stood waiting for him. We had been pushed out of the old chocolate factory before seven as usual and it was a rough start to the day as there was no place to take shelter. After a few minutes under the drizzling rain shower, my clothes were wet through. My stomach began rumbling with hunger and my body shivered in the cold air. I started coughing and spitting out which made me feel nauseous. Yalla eventually arrived from a direction I hadn't expected him to. He was not a member of our night shelter. I had never known him spend a single night there which made me curious as to where he did sleep. From what I observed in the Dune life, the Frailty for Strength was the only place where an illegal alien could safely pass the night. I reminded myself that Yalla had lived in the Dune for twenty-six years and was unlikely to be in need of my concern.

Yalla looked bright and happy when he appeared and

greeted me with a warm handshake and I decided that he must have spent the night under a thicker blanket than I had.

"You see Eba, it is raining but the sun is shining at the same time." He spoke with delight as if he was trying to further cajole me into accepting the sunset theory he'd shared with me the previous evening.

"Yes sure," I agreed, in order to preserve the geniality between us.

"That sounds hopeful, let's go," he urged me as we took the route towards the east end of town.

After climbing the thirty-three steps that led the way to Yalla's friend's office, I was nervous and started to reconsider whether my decision to go there with Yalla had been a wise one. When we reached the main door, I stepped behind Yalla who rang the doorbell several times. The door was finally opened and a bright light was flashed in our faces by a chubby man with a sweaty bald head. The man was little more than five feet tall but his body was physically muscular and his broad face shone with humour. My first impression of him was that he didn't look dangerous.

"Yalla my friend! Why are you so early knocking on my door this morning?" He hugged Yalla and laughed loudly. I could see from his eyes that the two men were well connected to each other and their first exchange of words in my presence reignited my smile.

After he was done with hugging Yalla, I gave him a kind handshake and a broad smile.

"Welcome, come inside," he said kindly as he led us through the little dark hallway to his office.

"And you are? What's your name?" he asked me.

"My name is Eba," I answered with a shy expression.

"Sounds strong, your name," he replied insincerely before introducing himself.

"My name is Moelener, Sam Moelener, but you can call me Sam if you prefer." While Sam and I introduced ourselves, Yalla had already taken a seat on one of the green rubber stools in the canteen next to the office and was busy feasting on what looked like a leftover cheese sandwich. He looked comfortable with the surroundings in Sam Moelener's office. It was a little bit strange for me as I was just a newcomer. It was also the first time I had entered a person's private office in the year I had been in the Dune.

"Coffee or tea?" Sam asked me as he lifted some cups from a cupboard.

"Tea please," I replied. Yalla asked for a black coffee.

"Tea is for ladies, Eba," Sam scolded me light-heartedly.

"I do drink all kinds of coffee," I said, "but I prefer to have coffee produced in my country." The rhythm and content of my words conveyed my national pride.

Sam winked at me and said, "Good for you if you say so, Eba. Everyone is proud of their home-made produce. Here in the Promised Land we are proud that we produce the best wine in the whole world." I thought of my uncle who used to claim that the best coffee in the world came from our country. During my time in the Dune, I had never seen the local coffee from my country for sale in the markets, and the only things I had heard people mention about our country was the war and the dictatorship regime in power.

"Eba, what was it that brought you here to the Promised Land anyway, if I may ask?" Sam studied me as he questioned me but continued speaking before I had the chance to respond.

"Mining ambitions, problems or is it for a brighter future?"

"It's a long story, sir. I don't like to talk about it."

I used the word 'sir' when I spoke to Sam because he looked like a man who was as old as my father.

"Here you have rights to choose what you would like to tell, Eba. This is a free country." I detected a sarcastic tone in his comment.

I learned from Yalla that Sam Moelener, who would be fifty-seven years of age the following month, was a local politician who represented a small constituency inside the Promised Land. With the support of the local council, he had set up a humanitarian foundation called 'Clean It Up' which declared its purpose in its mission statement as being "to care for and heal the people of the Dune district." During our conversation, Sam told me about how he had started his organisation with a campaign to eradicate street begging within the district of the Dune.

A campaign which he claimed was a huge success as begging on the streets was subsequently forbidden according to the laws of the community. He also organised programmes to raise the necessary funds to support people in need, but only through his organisation. It seemed to me that Sam's goal was to contain all beggars under one umbrella, like the union of beggars. It was a notion which helped to keep the streets clean according to Sam who told me, "I chose to come down here to the Dune and set up my private office so I could interact teeth and tongue with illegal aliens in desperate need."

Sam's foundation was not the only one operating in the Dune, there were other organisations that had similar goals to his. All were there to help, but there was a secret rivalry between the helpers of the different organisations. I was baffled when I heard about the rivalry as I couldn't figure out why people with the same mission would want to fight each other if it was not in the interest of financial gain. A world which vowed to stand up and help the poor, in my view, had become a world full of doubt and had a lot of hidden dirt under its carpets.

After our drink, as we prepared to leave, Sam said to me, "Eba, you can always come to me and ask for anything you may need."

"Thank you, Sam," I replied as I shook his hand again, "I have to leave for the night shelter now." Yalla and I left the building together.

No one answered the doorbell at the night shelter, even after I'd rung it several times. It was a quarter past ten in the evening in the middle of an ice-cold winter. The streets were already covered with piles of white snow, and heavy snowflakes were still pouring down.

I was late and the only night shelter in the Dune was closed. I had been caught out by the rules. The doors of the night shelter were only open between nine and ten in the evening, and only for registered sleepers.

I couldn't hold back my tears when I realised they were not going to let me in, and my breaking tears gave way to a broken heart as I was terrified about prospect of sleeping outside on such a cold night. It was a degree of suffering which I thought I didn't deserve, but couldn't do anything about. I decided it must have been Mr Stein, the old military veteran, who was in charge at the shelter that night, as if it had been the old Willie I knew she would have opened that door widely and let me in.

I tried to figure out where I could go and shelter for the night. I knew it was my fault. I should have gone straight to the night shelter when I left Sam's office, but instead I'd stopped at a live music concert Sam and Yalla had talked about earlier that afternoon. The band were performing in the evenings at the town square in a benefit concert to raise funds for supporting illegal aliens. I thought about going back to Sam's office in case he might still be there, but I remembered hearing him telling Yalla that he was going to watch a football match that evening. He'd said, "I also have to leave early today, I am just waiting for you two to leave." Reflecting back on Sam's words gave me the impression he would not be returning to his office that night.

I couldn't think of any way to find a roof that I could keep my head safely under for the night. I tried to figure out where Yalla might be at that moment. I thought it was too cold and late for him to be at the boulevard. Being locked outside in the cold made me feel foolish for never having asked Yalla where he stayed.

I walked away to look for a dwelling place for the night. After a few steps I stopped to look back at the footprints I'd left behind, clearly stamped in the snow. I decided to walk all the way to the abandoned railway station which I'd once stumbled across when exploring the Dune. The old railway station was a flat building, secured with large wooden doors at the front and a couple of narrow glass windows on the side. In spite of the dangers on the streets late at night I set off towards the old railway station. When I arrived I saw the place was fully occupied by squatters, some lying on thin mattresses and others on folded cardboard boxes. As I went deeper into the building, I noticed a family of four huddled together. Mother, father and two children were in a deep sleep, snoring like tired manual labourers. I had assumed I would be the only squatter in the old train station that night, and I certainly hadn't expected it to be such a busy place. This discovery made me doubt whether my decision to go there had been a good one, and also made me realise that there were many others who were as desperate for a roof over their head as I was.

It was eerily quiet inside the dark railway waiting hall, a quietness which reminded me of the silence of a graveyard.

There was no extra bedding or sheet covers around so, shivering more intensely with each breath, I lowered my body onto the bare floor and rested my head on my backpack.

A man lying next to me threw a blanket to me and whispered, "Take this". At that moment I considered him to be the good Samaritan. I looked at him but I couldn't make out his facial features as the whole building was in darkness. There was no electricity in the building so the only source of light was from the reflection of the old seaport. I made myself as comfortable as I could on the hard floor and fell into my slumber. I couldn't remember the exact moment I entered the rapid eye movement session of my sleeping journey.

The next morning it was freezing. I walked the streets again and looked for Yalla at our usual meeting point. Strangely, Yalla hadn't showed up after I had waited for an hour. I waited for another hour but he still didn't show up so I decided to go over to Sam's place to see if he knew where he was. At Sam's office, I found Yalla. He was feasting on a large toasted cheese sandwich and a cup of coffee. He looked relaxed and comfortable on the wooden dining chair.

"Would you like to have one of these?" he asked me hastily, raising what was left of his sandwich.

"Yes sure," I answered without hesitation.

After Yalla had finished his sandwich, he went into the kitchen and prepared a cheese sandwich for me just like his. Sam was busy in his office attending to other visitors.

Yalla and I were treated like special guests in Sam's office, the benefit extended to me due to Sam's respect for Yalla. The special way Sam treated us compared to others sometimes left me curious about the relationship between Sam and Yalla, which looked like a very close one.

"Here you go," Yalla said as he served me the toasted cheese sandwich.

With the kindness and services of Yalla, I felt like a lucky man. I felt blessed to have met someone like him in such a dumping hole as the Dune. At least I had the feeling of being safe and secure during the day whenever I sat in Sam's office. On that morning, after being left outside in the wilderness the previous night, and in the middle of a brutal winter, Sam Moelener was added to my list of people I was grateful to.

"Eat well and put on warm clothing before you get swallowed by the cold," Yalla warned me. I pretended not to hear what he said and just continued eating my sandwich. But he didn't ignore me despite my mean attitude, and continued to tell me his life story.

"When I arrived here at the Promised Land I was just like you, Eba. No friends, no shelter, no hope. I had to start all over again, a new day, a new life." He paused and took a sip from his coffee cup. "When I was rejected by the computer system of the Promised Land, the world became smaller for me. After a few years I met Sam, and when he listened to my story he felt pity for me. He connected me to work underground at the pig slaughterhouse in the Dune, which was then the only place where an illegal alien could find a job. People said I was one of the lucky ones. I worked damn hard for ten hours a day, seven days a week, but received a pay equivalent to one-third of the minimum wage of a normal citizen of the Promised Land. I knew it was unfair, but I had to take it. I had to make a living."

"Life is not fair" I murmured as I rolled my tongue around my mouth to clear the remnants of sticky cheese left between my wisdom teeth.

"Yes, life is indeed not fair," Yalla nodded his head and continued to tell me about his misfortunes. He was shaking as he spoke. "I slaughtered hundreds of pigs with those sharp blades at the slaughterhouse. I watched pig heads rolling in huge numbers, that makes me feel emotional sometimes while I am working. Species taking the lives of other living species just to make a living. Life is certainly unfair, Eba." I saw a tear forming as he continued telling me about his life experience in the Promised Land.

"People come here in different ways, and for different reasons," Yalla said, "I left my home town, a warm and beautiful place, in search of a treasure. My friends and family used to tell me the story of the treasure which they say was stolen from us long ago by men with blades and taken to a place called the Promised Land. My expectations were higher than the sky and tempted me to take the adventure, even when I didn't have the means. As a young man at the time, I did what I had to do. I endured all the difficulties during my journey to come here, with the hope that I could simply find pieces of that stolen treasure and take it back home to share with my family." He turned his face to the wall, giving me the impression that he felt guilty about something. After a few seconds he turned back to me and continued.

"But Eba," he said as he looked directly into my eyes, "I understand that you are in search of the Hundred Golden Horses. Maybe there is a treasure somewhere in the Promised Land, but I believe that it is not visible, you could never see it. The story of the stolen treasure is a fairy tale. Perhaps it is true that the treasure was stolen during the golden ages, but I believe that the treasure was melted and used to build the infrastructure of the Promised Land. If you take a look at the city inside the walls of the Promised Land it is beautiful, isn't it? It looks like diamond, gold and silver, doesn't it?" He was clearly emotional as he asked me those questions and he looked at me directly as he continued to impart his advice.

"Eba, make sure you live a life that is measurable. We all have dreams in this life but try to figure out what is the reality in realising your dreams. Guarantee yourself you won't write your dreams on a castle stone, make sure you write your dreams on a piece of paper so you can always rewrite them whenever you have to take another turn in life. Let me tell you another thing Eba, I am tired of living this life. If I die here on the streets of the Promised Land, tell everyone that it is not my fault, it happened because of the system." Yalla's story and the advice he gave me were moving. I felt ashamed of being a human being, ashamed of the harmful way humans had treated one of their own kind. I wanted to manifest into a million men who could make a positive change in the lives of someone like Yalla, and maybe many others. It was an emotional day for me and Yalla. A day which we decided to spend together at Sam's office. We had good conversation throughout the day, but I remembered to leave early for the night shelter, a lesson I learned from a man I once called my mentor.

The day after Yalla had vented his frustrations, when I came out of the shelter, the ground was all white and it was snowing hard that I could barely move through the piles of snow on the street. My jacket wasn't thick enough to hold the melting ice as it drained into my clothes, soaking me through to the skin. My fingers were frozen as I approached the door of Sam's office. It was almost impossible to press the doorbell as my fingers were so stiff I could barely move them.

I heard someone calling my name from the street and, when I turned around to see who it was, I saw Sam hurrying towards his office. He looked stressed and when he got closer I could see that his face was red.

"Is Yalla here already?" I asked Sam as he opened the door for us. He shook his head and stared at me. "Good things don't last long, Eba, just like the way good people are born into this world, serve their purpose and then leave." He lowered his head and looked down at the floor.

"What does that mean, Sam?"

"Your friend, our friend, Yalla, was found early this morning inside an abandoned building, hanging naked with a static climbing rope knotted around his throat, dead. I was contacted by the internal affairs committee of the Promised Land. I am sorry, Eba." He didn't look up from the floor as he spoke in a sorrowful, low voice.

A cold shiver ran up my body as I digested Sam's announcement. Yalla was not my real family in terms of bloodline, but he was someone who I had connected with and believed in. A man who I didn't only learn a lot from, but also trusted so much. His words had helped me to open my eyes and see the reality of the situation in which I had found myself. For me, Yalla was a symbol of hope and courage, a man who was honest enough to share his mistakes with others so they would not fall victim to a similar fate. His wisdom and experience had been the only hope I had of finding my way back home.

The news of Yalla's death left me weeping. I began to feel the pain of losing a friend who had cared so much for my wellbeing. Yalla's death made me weep openly for the first time in my adult life. I wondered whether I would go through the same pain he had endured. Yalla's end was like a rusty dagger, full of disappointment, being stabbed into the heart of his dreams and manifesting into a poisonous tetanus which slowly spread to his brain and caused him to take his own life.

After I had recovered a little from the initial shock of the sad news, Sam tapped me on my shoulder and asked me to join him for a cup of coffee.

Inside his office, he explained more about how Yalla's body was going to be cremated. He said Yalla didn't have a permit or insurance for his body to be repatriated back to his home country, or to be buried properly in a grave in the Dune. This upset me deeply because Yalla had once told me that he would like, when he passed away, to be buried in a grave. Even if there was a way to return his body back to his home, that would have been impossible as we had no details with which to trace his family.

As we drank our coffee Sam said to me, "Yalla was a good friend of mine too, I am sorry that his body is going to be cremated this afternoon at the crematorium." I began to think about the implications of Yalla's story on my own future and wondered what they would do with my body if I died here as an illegal alien. The traditions in Yalla's place of birth are similar to mine as we came from neighbouring countries. In our tradition, it is forbidden for someone's body to be cremated, even if it is a stranger's. We always bury the dead. I believed that Yalla's body and soul would not be pleased with the way he was going to be laid to rest. When I recalled the challenging conversation I'd had the previous day with Yalla, my mind reflected back to his mood at the time as he explained the disappointments he had faced in the Promised Land. I suspected he knew what he was saying, and had already made a resolution to end his own life in such a tragic way. I could see images of the sour expression on his face which was so different than his usual cheerful disposition. His manner during our conversation the day before had concerned me after we had separated, as it was clear that something was wrong. He seemed to be tired with life, as if he had given up.

I told myself that Yalla's death should serve me as a lesson about life, and that I should consider his struggle and experience as food for thought. A wise man once said to me that it is important to learn from the mistakes of your elders so that one day you can teach your own children, so they will not repeat the same mistakes.

Sam came to me later at the main hall in his office with a document which he read aloud.

Yalla Banke - an illegal gold miner who henceforth, according to the laws of the Promised Land and the powers of his majesty the king, has been granted the status of a legal miner who, according to the law, has the legitimacy and rights of the citizens of the above mentioned land.

Following his tragic death, the body of the deceased has claimed the full rights to be cremated today at three o'clock in the afternoon at the St. Shabrina Holy Cemetery.

All friends and acquaintances are welcome.

Regards from his contact person, Sam Moelener.

Sam folded the document, looked at me and said, "I was his contact person. All his personal affairs were under my watch." Rather abruptly he then asked me to leave because, he informed me, he was heading for the mortuary to arrange the cremation ceremony of his friend.

The Neighbourhood Watch was a force to be reckoned with as far as citizens living in the walls were concerned. A force for good which carried the powers given to its operation by the king himself. The King of the Promised Land had equipped them with the rights and mandates to search door to door and remove what he described as illegal aliens from the Dune. They were busy searching a man on the road right ahead of me when I accidentally ran into their check point. I spotted them wrestling a weak and tired looking man who fought hard as he tried to stop them from putting his wrists in handcuffs. The four gigantic Neighbourhood Watch men were trained to deal with, and take control of, such kind of awkward situations.

As they struggled with the man, who I believed was an illegal alien just like me, I made myself look small and confidently passed through the checkpoint just like any normal citizen would. My pretence felt magical as I passed through the guards' checkpoint without challenge. I looked the other way as if I had no interest in the ongoing confrontation between the guards and their suspect. I survived the check that day, but it left me with a heavy heart. Those were the kind of situations I had to worry about every day, it was heart-rending.

My late friend Yalla once told me about when he was arrested by the Neighbourhood Watch when they found him working illegally at the slaughterhouse. He was caught during a general check. His arrest raised the alarm that he was an illegal alien and, when his status had been confirmed, he was taken away and locked in a high security prison where he served eighteen months without trial or bail. He was locked up because he had been cast out as an illegal alien who worked for three times less than the normal wage just to make a living, he had told me.

I was anxious every time I thought about Yalla's story and found myself in an almost constant state of fear, especially during the times I wandered the streets of the Dune.

The next day Sam, together with some other friends of Yalla's, organised a vigil inside the main hall at Sam's office. Most of those who attended were illegal aliens. We lit candles in the formation of a heart which signified a symbol of our love, respect and compassion for our deceased friend. People prayed for him in their own ways. When I looked around at them I saw a lost community. A community of lost humans who spent their lives fighting to survive in a foreign land without a voice. A misfortunate generation of treasure seekers who had lost their human social rights and wellbeing. A generation which I later realised was sillier than those who went earlier to the pyramids in search of the holy grail.

After the vigil, Sam came to join me where I was sitting and drew a stool close to mine.

"You are not alone, Eba. I am right here with you. I will look after you just as I did for Yalla before he passed away."

"Thank you, Sam," I replied. His words ignited a little joy inside me, a joy which suppressed my tears for a few minutes.

To most of the people in the room, Sam appeared to be a generous man. His benevolence often provoked my curiosity. I had been through some terrible experiences, particularly the events in the house of Samir El Sheik, and having reflected on what had happened between Samir and me I had become much more sceptical about the people I met. Consequently, although Sam was kind to me, I still had my doubts about him.

After the service we settled down as a group to have dinner, which was followed by a prayer ceremony. The priest arrived dressed in a double gown and wearing a pair of brown leather sandals. He held a long rosary in his right hand and counted its beads as he prayed. During the prayers, I noticed an angry-looking man who I supposed also had the difficult life of being an illegal alien in the Dune. He looked frustrated, not only by Yalla's death but also about the inhumane treatment taking place in the so-called civilised world. The man interrupted the prayers and began cursing the priest. The priest calmly continued with the prayers each time the man tried to say something weird, but the man interrupted and cursed the priest again. The man looked like someone who had been lost in the jungle for a long time, and didn't seem to care about his bushy red beard which looked like it hadn't been shaved in years. The smell from his beard, and from his hair which dropped into natural dreadlocks, wasn't pleasant to inhale. The man started yelling, "There is no God here, we are tired of hearing all the preaching about hope. We need a solution to this right now. We are also humans!" The man raised his arms and let out a bitter cry.

When the man was done with exercising his anger, the priest walked over to him and, taking him into a gentle embrace, said to him, "Son, you have been forgiven. I understand why all of this is so heart-breaking. But there is always a way for those who have faith in themselves and in God." The priest continued with his prayers without any further disturbance.

The weather that day was much better than it had been on the previous days and Sam and I decided to go to the seaside to walk along the boulevard, in an attempt to rid ourselves of our emotions following the dreadful departure of our friend Yalla Banke.

"What are your plans from here, Eba?" Sam asked as we sat on the same spot where I used to sit with Yalla.

I couldn't answer his question. It seemed like I was caught in the middle of a crossfire. At that moment I was unable to think lucidly about getting out of there, let alone work out how I was going to do it.

"You have no rights to find a job and work, to walk on the streets of the Promised Land or to have an education."

"I know, Sam. But for now I have to figure out what I should do as the way back home is closed."

"I feel pity for people in your situation, Eba. You have to hide behind the curtains for a long time, perhaps for the rest of your life, just like our late friend Yalla." He looked at me, as if waiting for my response, but I didn't say a word as the subject weighed too heavily on my back. Sam continued, "Come to my office next week, Eba. I'll try to find you a job."

"I will do," I replied. We said our goodbyes and went our separate ways.

One week later at Sam's office, I found myself overcome with nerves as I sat on the single sofa chair waiting to be invited into his office. I wasn't the only person in my situation who Sam helped, there was always a long queue of people waiting to see him at his office.

"You can come inside now, Eba," Sam said as he waved me into his office.

"I have a job for you at the stone quarry. It will suit you I think," Sam offered.

"I will do anything in order to earn a living," I replied as quickly as I could in case Sam changed his mind. I was desperate to have a job I could make a genuine living out of.

"Good, Eba. You can start tomorrow without a job interview."

I worked in the Central Locomotory Quarry, known as the C.L.Q., which was the only quarry surviving from the stone mining industry which had once been so important in the history of the Promised Land. Even though it catered for the lowest working class, it was still an enviable position for someone in my situation. The quarry was the size of two football fields, though it was clear that its facilities were outdated. We used dynamite and other explosives to drill and blast the mighty rocks hanging right above the manual labourers. When I arrived there on my first day of work I nearly turned down the offer, but my second thought saved the day. The mine wardens were mostly old men who had worked in the quarry business all their lives and they had a brutal and merciless attitude towards their labourers. One of them said to me, "Be careful young man, I am tired of seeing dead bodies around, you better put on your boots and helmet right now before you get fired." The warden had a long Fu Manchu moustache threaded above his lips and running down to his chin. Even though his long, cocaine nose was covered with a mask, I could still make it out. The loud noise of explosives at close range hurt my eardrums and the dust from the stones after they were ground left me coughing in my sleep at night. I could also see evidence of labourers with tuberculosis when they coughed and spat out bloody saliva. Because I had no other realistic options, I held on and survived in that pit hole in the middle of the quarry, carrying ground stones in a wheelbarrow which I had to fill with a shovel. My palms became harder than those of my father when he tilled the land and planted root vegetables. But the work at the quarry gave me the chance to make a better life for myself in the Dune, not a good life but certainly a better one.

After working at the quarry for three months, I realised I had saved a reasonable sum of money at Sam's. We had agreed that I should save my money at his office as it was the only place it would be in safe hands, as I wasn't allowed to have an account at the bank. No legal job and no bank account, in accordance with the law. I suspected that Sam had done the same for Yalla and many others, saving their cash in his office safe. I had seen him opening that safe a few times when he had given me some money, but I reckoned the code of that giant black till changed each and every time. With my new job, I could afford to buy a proper meal at least once a day at the only restaurant in the Dune which delivered their services through a mobile food on wheels caravan cab. Being able to have some choice on whether, and what, I ate for a meal was a distinct improvement, but life itself had yet to become normal. I had to work seven days a week for only a quarter of the minimum wage, the same bleak contract Yalla had complained about. The contract was like a sugar-coated bitter pill which was hard to swallow, but it was better than having nothing to heal my extreme suffering.

My friendship with Sam gradually became more intimate until he asked me one evening, "Would you like to come with me to the nude beach this weekend?"

"What do they do there?" I asked uncertainly.

"People go there to relax and make new friends,"

"I can't do that, Sam. I feel too much shame to expose my body. Besides, according to our tradition it is forbidden to walk around completely naked amongst other people."

"Ok, good for you Eba," Sam said as he looked at me with a bemused expression.

My habit of not trusting strangers was exacerbated by
the hard lessons I'd learned during my journey in the desert and in the abandoned city. But on the other hand I remembered what Yalla had once advised me on the subject of
trust. "Don't trust this world and its people too readily. Open
a little window of trust and get to know people better before
you open your front door."

I found his advice on trusting people confusing and wasn't
confident that I had really understood his meaning. People
often threw words of advice to me but it was down to me to
choose the best advice to heed in order to improve my life.

It was two years since I had left my land, but nothing had
changed for the better. Life in the Promised Land was tough
like a solid and mighty rock which I must use my bare hands
to pierce through in order for me to see the beauty inside.

Sam had become increasingly demanding of me during
the last year. One cold evening, we were in his office doing
checks and balances on my savings account when he offered me a massage. He said I had to take off my clothes and
lay naked on top of the long dining table in the kitchen. It
struck me as a strange offer. In my tradition, people only got
massaged by traditional doctors when they were seriously
ill or in severe pain. The traditional healers in my country
didn't give massages by stripping another man naked on top
of a dining table.

The moment I refused Sam's offer of a massage was the
moment the bond between us started to break. I noticed his
countenance change as he stood up from his office chair,
opened his eyes wide and spread his hands aggressively.

I made a swift judgment and started making my way out of

the office before history could repeat itself.

"I have to leave now, Sam."

"Stop Eba!" Sam yelled at me and drew a long silver kitchen knife from one of the drawers of his desk and held it towards me. I edged towards the door of his office before he could make a move or get any closer. I was frightened by the thundering sound of his voice. I tried to assess his mood and saw that his face had crumpled. Despite my fear, I continued to double my steps down the stairs without looking backwards. I could hear the clicks made by Sam's leather boots as he chased me down the stairs. He lost ground on me due to his poor physical condition and started yelling at me in a desperate voice, "You can't run away from me, Eba. You know how much I love you. This was how things used to work between poor Yalla and me." We both stopped on the stairs for a moment, enough steps between us for me to be sure he couldn't reach me. He held the knife tightly in his hand as he continued yelling.

"Do you think you can get away with this after all the things I have done for you, Eba? You have to pay me back, you owe me."

"I owe you nothing, Sam!" I replied. "You can take all the money you have been saving for me and get out of my life, I don't want to see you again!" The echoes of my name being shouted as I raced down the stairs couldn't change a thing and I didn't waste more time. I took off again on my heels, as desperate as a rat trying to survive the deadly claws of a well-trained and experienced hunting cat. Sam didn't give up and he chased me down the stairs. I quickened my pace again and lost control of my step as my whole body capsized onto the floor and I rolled down the stairs. I landed at the wide door, the main entrance to the building, which I ran through. As I ran I heard Sam shouting to me from the doorway.

"I know where to find you, Eba! I will find you and hand you over to the Neighbourhood Watch after I'm finished with you. I will tell them that you are an illegal alien." I had heard enough of his threats and continued to run. The pain in my right leg was excruciating, but I had to endure it to get out of the area while I still could.

Love And Affection

'Doctors without borders' was a clinic set up in a huge tent and was the only clinic in the Dune. They were a voluntary organisation of passionate medical volunteers and professionals, who had dedicated their lives to saving others. They came to the Dune to help people in my situation. The credibility of the organisation was recognised and they were trusted by the people after twenty-five years of medical services to the poor of the Dune. If I ever have an opportunity to award a medal for philanthropy I would surely award the medal to that organisation.

After escaping from Sam, I went immediately to the clinic which was the only place where I could receive free medical treatment for my injured leg. With so much pain in my leg I had to drag myself slowly to the doctors.

It was busy in the clinic when I arrived, limping heavily on one leg. I was received gracefully by an old nurse who took me to a camp bed and told me to wait for the doctor, who would be along to attend to me shortly.

"Relax, young man," said a young, soothing female voice shortly after the old nurse had left. She was the doctor.

"You are now in good hands," she comforted me, with a broad smile on her face which made the shape of a small, glittering diamond.

"I am going to examine you to find out whether you have

broken a bone, and tomorrow one of my colleagues will tell you the results." she told me. Our eyes met as she pressed her stethoscope against different parts of my body. She listened to my heartbeat and my lungs and then examined the wound on my lower leg. She also asked for a blood sample to check for STDs. She said I didn't have to explain how I got injured unless I wanted to. I preferred not to tell her about everything that had happened between me and Sam, and instead said only that I had fallen down the stairs at a friend's house. The doctors there were professionally trained to understand the plight of people in situations like mine, and by not pushing for information they showed their respect for the boundaries and privacy of their patients.

Having examined me, the doctor laid my head on a pillow and covered me with a grey blanket before she left silently. I could still feel the spark left behind when her deep blue eyes met my big brown ones. I wondered whether I would ever lay my ambitious eyes on her again or not. I was admitted to the clinic for the night. I hoped the doctor would show up again that day but, much to my disappointment, when someone did come back it was the old nurse who had received me earlier. She checked on me frequently with a great deal of kindness. She tirelessly asked me how I was feeling and brought my medication with a cocktail of assorted fruits. She said to me, "Eat, because food is an important part of healing." I ate all the fruit she offered me.

The green stretcher I lay on had stains of dried blood drops on it. It looked like it was an old bed which had rescued many victims before me. Lying on that stretcher, I had the feeling that my injured leg would heal thanks to the treatment I had received.

"Mr Eba Yoko," a jovial voice called from the corridor near the clinic's main entrance. When I turned, I saw her coming towards my bed with a black file holding a stack of paper.

"Here are the results of the various tests and samples we took from you yesterday."

When she got closer I noticed the name-tag attached to her chest. Doctor E.D. Islaker. It was the blue-eyed doctor who had treated me the previous day, the blue eyes I'd longed to see again. Her last name caught my attention. It sounded familiar, a name I felt sure I had come across before, and I remembered it was the name of the doctor who had rescued me after the boat accident a few years earlier. The blue-eyed doctor interrupted my thoughts as she began to explain the contents of the medical report. She told me I hadn't broken the bone, it was only a minor injury which would heal within a few days, and that I had no STDs or malaria. This time she seemed more relaxed than she had the previous day when we first met. I was surprised that she had showed up, as I had expected one of her colleagues to bring the test results. I dared for the second time to look straight into her eyes while she read the report. When she had finished, she looked up and our eyes met. Mine suddenly became hot, like fire. She smiled and asked, "Any questions, Mr Yoko?"

"Not really," I said, "I am just curious about your last name on your tag, Islaker."

"That name is actually from my mother," she replied.

"It is the same name as one of the doctors who rescued me from a boat accident a few years ago. Her name was Doctor Islaker too, and it was spelled exactly the same way as yours." I looked at her inquisitively.

"My mother is also a medical doctor. She is a volunteer at the coastal rescue medical team. So, you never know, it might have been my mom," she replied.

I had no doubt that her mother had been my rescuer and asked myself whether crossing paths with the daughter of the person who had saved my life could just be a coincidence. If it was, it must have happened for a good reason.

"I have to discharge you now, Mr Yoko, you are good to go, and I hope we will meet again," said Doctor Islaker. When she turned her back to leave, a blank sheet of paper dropped from her file onto the floor. She didn't notice it and kept walking as my eyes leapt onto what could be the last opportunity I had to grab her attention. My stomach was filled with butterflies as I prepared to put down the heavy load which I had carried for the last twenty-four hours. I wondered whether she was also carrying something similar within her, or maybe wearing pink glasses on her precious face.

"Miss Islaker," I called with a shaky voice, "you've dropped something." When she turned around, her long brown hair flipped and twisted and landed on her shoulder. She smiled and walked back to me.

"Thank you," she said with a broad smile. I could feel a connection between us as the solid ice which kept her in her comfort zone was broken. She smiled warmly as I was about to hand her the fallen piece of paper, which gave me the courage to demand more attention. I held on to the piece of paper a little more firmly, so that she had to pull it away from my fingers. That was my moment and I put it to good use with the affectionate play with the paper. When she managed to remove the piece of paper from my grip, she paused and looked at me with a deliberate stare which reminded me of a flirting love bird, making her intentions clear in a playful way. She took a pen from the pocket of her navy-blue scrubs and wrote something on the blank piece of paper which we had wrestled over before gently handing it to me. She turned on her heels and left without speaking a word. I'd noticed one of her colleagues, a tall woman with a long chin, closely observing the interaction between us. On my way out of the clinic, the woman approached me and whispered into my ear, "Go and get her." She rolled her eyes clockwise and went back to her work. My heart beat faster as I considered the possibility that something good was hanging on the horizon.

There is nothing worse than someone who is running away from one problem then having the misfortune to fall into another. I always had to raise my neck high and look back like a frightened flamingo guarding her chicks against a predatory attack. That was how I spent my days, turning back and looking for someone following me along the streets of the Dune. My new challenge was to hide from Sam Moelener, a new burden which threatened to tear me apart. I was like new-born buffalo calf running away to survive a deadly lion hunt.

Sam Moelener was a well-known social organiser who had earned a good name for his benevolence, especially when it came to helping illegal aliens. He was a household name in the Dune, a name written at the top of a list of good doers, and his name was on the lips of almost every inhabitant of the Dune. It was a pity that many of those people had no idea what he was truly like on the inside. I had the same impression of him when we first met and believed he had good intentions from the comforting way he talked to people. I saw an angel who had been sent in the form of a man in order to set people free from injustice and hunger. My first impressions of Sam were so positive I couldn't have imagined during my early days in the Dune that his seemingly magical qualities would turn out to become another disappointment in my life. He turned out just like Samir, a daydream nightmare.

After leaving the clinic, I wandered the streets to pass the time. As I approached the boulevard, I felt raindrops on my face. The shower became heavier and the raindrops formed holes as they landed on the unpaved road. The intensity of the rain forced me to run as fast as I could to shelter myself under the roof of an old building. While I waited for the rain to stop, a brown and black striped Beagle appeared, breathing hard through its half-opened mouth. The stray dog stopped and joined me as we shared the plight of seeking a dry shelter. Sharing the same roof with my new Beagle friend, I felt a sheet of paper in the front pocket of my blue denims when I wiped my wet hands on them. At first, I thought it was some cash which I had forgotten about, but on the other hand I never carried so much money that I could forget some of it in my pocket. As I dipped my hand into my right pocket I realised it was the note, presumably a medicine prescription, that the doctor had given me before I left the clinic. The piece of paper was folded when I took it out and half soaked due to the downpour of rain. I took my time and began to carefully unfold the paper. The words, written in blue ink, read, "It was nice meeting you, Eba. I am going to ask my mother to confirm. Let us meet tomorrow under the Dune bridge at 17:30 hours. I will surely be there. Take care of yourself. Hugs and kisses, Elena."

After reading the note my world turned around, though I couldn't figure out what the outcome of our meeting would be. My whole body became cold and my lips trembled for a while. I asked myself if she was an angel or just another dream. It was hard to believe that this could happen to someone like me, an ordinary illegal alien roaming the streets of the Dune, a place hope itself had long since said goodbye to, with nothing. After the ice breaker at the clinic, I sensed something was hanging on the horizon, something I couldn't imagine.

At five o'clock the following day, a cold afternoon, I stood under the old Dune bridge built purely with iron. It had been exactly twenty-four hours since I had read Elena's note. I still had some nervous thirty minutes to endure before I could see her and I was restlessly walking back and forth around the perimeter where I expected her to emerge. As I waited, my imagination was in another world. A world where love and affection would be the leaders, where people could love only by true choice rather than force. My fears of running away from people like Sam Moelener and the Neighbourhood Watch were conquered. During the past twenty-four hours such images hadn't crossed my mind. The power of falling in love had taken over and I had thought of nothing but Elena all day and night.

I was startled by a car horn unexpectedly sounding a double tone loudly and clearly in the distance. As I turned around, I saw two beautiful women and I could tell, even from a distance, that they resembled each other in many ways such as their height, hair colour and build.

"Eba!" Elena called.

She waved at me and beckoned me over to the grey Mini on which they were both leaning. I became as urgent as a late-night fox as I took double steps towards them. As soon as I reached them, Elena gave me a broad smile and told me to jump into the car. I quickly grabbed the handle of the rear passenger door and pulled it open. It felt comfortable inside as I rested myself on the perfectly upholstered back seat. Elena looked delighted as our first official meeting began to unfold. Once settled inside the car, I shut the door and Elena started the engine and we took off. Only then did I look properly at Elena's companion who I recognised immediately as Doctor Islaker senior. The honorary lady hadn't changed at all, she looked just the same as she had when I first saw her after they rescued me.

"Nice to meet you again, Eba," she said with a genuine warmth.

"It is my pleasure, Doctor Islaker," I replied.

The sentimental music on the radio might have made Doctor Islaker senior cry a little, as I could see her face in the car's rear-view mirror. Tears ran down her cheeks while Elena hit the gas pedal hard to rev the engine.

"You were one of only two people to survive that fatal boat accident," Doctor Islaker senior said through her tears. I felt her passion for saving lives. I was a young man, of about the same age as her own child, who was lost in the middle of the wilderness. I could relate her pain to that which my own mother would have felt had she still been alive. In Doctor Islaker senior, I saw the face of a mother who would save the world if she could. I wished we could send a signal to the radio DJ to stop playing those emotional songs, but Elena stepped in by re-tuning the radio station to another one which was playing something more upbeat.

"You have told me all about this Mom," cautioned Elena.

Her mother wiped her cheeks with a pocket tissue and smiled.

"This is a double rescue. At least I feel lucky to find you again, Eba."

"That's right Mom," her daughter sealed the deal.

Elena pulled into a parking mall in the city centre. She drove round and round all the way up to the seventh deck where she finally found a parking spot. She turned off the car engine and announced that we were going to have dinner at a restaurant in the neighbourhood. Elena's announcement gave me the feeling we were going to celebrate a double rescue and the reunion with her mother.

Hanging above the main entrance of the restaurant was a signboard reading 'Welcome to the Ideal Organic Restaurant' in green writing.

I was impressed by the stylish furnishings inside the restaurant. The walls were painted purple, with a white ceiling from which red ball lights hung, burning dimly. The smell from the open kitchen was of roasted peppered meat which mingled pleasantly with that of the aromatic coffee from the bar. It was the first time I had seen professional chefs in their white suits with their toque blanche hats on and long black aprons tied behind their waist. The smell of roasting meat reminded me of my Aunty Agnes's kitchen.

We chose a table close to the broad glass window where we could watch the sun going down across the beautiful restaurant garden which was decorated with exotic flowers and a sparkling fountain.

"Lord, why is it so beautiful? Lord, I have never been in a beautiful place like this before. Lord, is this natural?" I lost my sight and the attention of Elena while I whispered those questions. I then remembered what people used to say, that the Promised Land is a wonderland, almost a heaven. The view I stared at in the garden outside the restaurant was evidence that those people had been right. I was finally inside the walls for the very first time.

'Welcome to the real world,' I told myself. From my late friend Yalla Banke's point of view, the Promised Land was a Shangri-La, and I could see that it was true. I'd heard many unfortunate citizens of the Promised Land say that too. It was a perfect work of art created by men and decorated with melted treasure.

Rice with chicken curry was on the menu, which made me feel like a lottery winner. As far as my ancestors were concerned rice should rule the day, and that was one of the values they passed on to my generation. I wasted no time in ordering a big plate of it. The ladies both ordered a vegetarian meal. That was the first time in my life I had heard about vegetarians and I was curious. I politely threw questions to Doctor Islaker senior.

"Why do people become vegetarians?" I asked.

"I became a vegetarian not long after my graduation as a medical doctor at the medical college, when I returned from my first mission as a volunteer in the civil war of the land of Yougosoba. During my service in that mission, I saw a lot of horrible things like human flesh, bodies so to speak. Since then I haven't eaten any form of meat again."

"I inherited it from her," Elena interrupted her mother,

with a smile on her face as usual. "Doctor Islaker," I said, grabbing the attention of the senior doctor again.

"I was born and raised during the civil war in Yougosoba."

"Oh really?" she asked, looking astonished with lines cutting across her forehead.

"Yes," I confirmed, "as a toddler I was informed that my mother was killed during an attack."

"That's a pity Eba," she comforted me, "Eat your food, one day you will find your mother living inside of somebody else."

Food was already being served as we discussed vegetarianism and the war. When I had read Elena's note the day before I had assumed that evening would be our first date, but unfortunately I had a more lengthy conversation with her mother, which separated Elena and me not in person but in spirit.

The food was delicious. I was surprised when I watched the Islaker women sharing the bill, which they split and paid equally. Elena seemed to notice my surprise and enlightened me on the subject.

"This is our tradition," she said, "don't be surprised."

"In my tradition, a man always foots the bill," I replied.

After a good evening of diverse conversation with the Islakers, an evening during which we learned more about each other, my hopes of seeing Elena again were not as high as they had been the previous day. I couldn't predict whether our future would just be a friendship or become an affectionate relationship. It felt as if they just wanted to know who I was and where I came from, and that was it, end of story. But when Elena dropped me off in the streets of the

Dune she got out of the car to give me a big hug and then reached for my cheeks which she kissed three times before sliding back into the driver's seat and driving off without another word.

My world came apart again after spending the evening in the company of those two beautiful souls. Their display of comfort and hope was unlike anything I had seen before, and ended with the touch of the hands and lips of the woman I was falling in love with.

The death of my friend and mentor Yalla left me lonely and I often just roamed the streets of the Dune like a vagabond. I became a bird without a destination, an abandoned beast from its own clan who was banished and left alone to suffer and die in the wilderness. Maybe I was too young to understand why Yalla decided to take his own life, because I couldn't figure out what could motivate a grown-up man to hang himself. On the other hand, had he still been alive I would have never known who Sam Moelener really was. It was only after Yalla's sorrowful departure that I began to realise the drive behind his mysterious death.

In our tradition, people would describe it not as a coincidence but a blessing which emerged from my grandmother's tomb. It was indeed a blessing to sit down at the same table as such beautiful and sympathetic women as the Islakers. Elena had arrived in my life at a time when I desperately needed someone to talk to and hold, a person who could teach me how to trust again. I wondered again whether she really was my true angel guardian, or whether this could be another nightmare in the making. My attraction to her had become a heavy storm which I couldn't stand, a storm which had swept me off my feet. The day after our meal at the restaurant it felt as if what had happened the previous evening was just a dream, fading away like smoke disappearing into the air. After the beautiful atmosphere in the restaurant, I was left all alone again to wander the streets. I didn't dare to go to the quarry as I had fired myself after the Sam Moelener saga.

I went to relieve myself inside a street mobile toilet built of hard plastic. During my excretions, I conjured up an image of Elena and I holding hands at the spot under the Dune bridge. My imaginations held me a bit too long inside the plastic cabin, a delay which annoyed the man who was waiting outside it. He ran out of patience and began knocking on the door angrily, which brought me back to reality. When I emerged from my fantasy world, I decided to fill my empty emotions by taking a walk to the Dune bridge, where I might feel like it's really happening. I couldn't figure out how I could find Elena again. Two hundred metres away from me I saw someone under the bridge, leaning on a grey car with both hands folded across their chest, but I couldn't make out who it was because the sky was already overshadowed by dusk. I began walking faster in order to have a closer look and saw that my instinct had been right. As I approached I saw the face and smile of a beautiful woman, Elena. Even before I reached for her embrace she had started to confess her feelings. "It just came into my mind and I took a gamble by coming here hoping I might find you, Eba," she said, "My heart told me if I came to the bridge I might find you again."

"I also felt the same about you, Elena," I admitted with a shaky voice.

During our confessions, I could feel the tenderness right

beyond the infinity of her heart as Elena's eyes were fixed on mine as if she was searching for the awakening of the hidden truth. I recognised a lustful desire in her eyes, the look of someone longing to hold another person's body in her sacred hands, and I knew I felt the same way. All my organs were burning inside of me as if they were not meant to be there. I was about to explode through the joy I felt as the sparks inside me couldn't hold on any more. The two and a half minutes for which we hugged was intense and intimate. I wrapped my hands gently around her lower back and she put one of her hands on my back and the other on my neck. I could feel the warmth of her palms like they were on fire. Our embrace expressed everything in its own way. It exposed the truth of how badly we needed each other, how long we had been craving for that moment to happen. After the longest hug I'd ever had, we released each other's body but still held hands as we looked searchingly into each other's eyes. I could see the tears of joy settling around Elena's heavenly eyes. With sighs of relief we gently reached for each other's lips, her upper lip in my mouth and her lower lip gently resting underneath mine. Her lips were rich and full, and the kiss lasted longer than I expected. It was a kiss which set me free, as free as a bird that had been locked in a cage for a very long time.

That was the first magical moment in my entire life. I, Eba Yoko, the son of an ordinary palm wine tapper, had kissed the most beautiful girl I had ever seen.

"I can't leave you here," Elena said, "come and stay with me in my apartment inside the walls of the Promised Land."

"I will go with you Elena," I agreed without hesitation.

We hugged each other again, both of us crying.

I was surprised by Elena's offer. I knew she was madly in love with me, and I with her, but I had not expected her to offer me a proper roof over my head inside the walls of the Promised Land. She did so despite it being forbidden by law for a citizen inside the walls to shelter an illegal alien.

That night when we went to bed we explored our different worlds. A stream of sensations flowed through our souls as we began to break through the boundaries which had suppressed our intimacy until then. The heavens fell down upon us, we heard angels singing sweet songs of healing. I will never forget those moments of my life.

"You are the first man to sleep in this bed," Elena said to me with a broad smile just after our first time in it.

"Well," I replied, "if that is true, lucky me." I gently traced the beautiful curves of her naked body with my finger as her head rested calmly on my bare chest. As I outlined the shape of a small love heart on her right shoulder, I was soothed into a long slumber.

The Unveiled Secrets

Since the evening I first entered Elena's apartment, my life took another trend. A trend which transformed me into a new man who people like Sam Moelener would never look at in the same way again.

After a month of living together, Elena extended her offer and invited me to stay with her permanently if I would like to. She provided the money for the groceries and I did the cooking. I cleaned the house, she washed the dishes. She paid all the bills. I played the role of bodyguard and house-keeper to her majesty.

One bright Sunday morning, while we were doing our normal once a week workout along the road, Elena asked me a question, "Promise me one thing, Eba."

"Just say it," I replied.

"Promise me that you will stop being afraid, and stop running away from the things and people that have troubled you?"

I paused and responded, "I will do as you ask, Elena." As she hugged me, she said soothingly, "From now on, put your trust in love, believe that love will always win." She smiled and took a deep sigh and we continued with the last few kilometres of our run.

That moment, when I made those promises to Elena, was the decisive moment in my new life, the moment I knew there was no turning back. From that point, I began to live my life in a proper, permanent home for the first time in three years. It was also my first experience of living with a partner. Living together with Elena felt good, but my soul was filled with many thoughts which made me feel ashamed of myself. I dwelled on how embarrassing it was for me to be unemployed and just sitting at home for the whole day, waiting for my partner to come home and cuddle me. Elena was the one who provided everything financially, a role I knew she played with a genuine intention. But on the other hand, Elena's extreme kindness to me made me feel vulnerable. I felt I wasn't fulfilling my responsibilities as a man. I wasn't fully satisfied with the role I played in the house even though Elena was. She often said to me, "Thank you for everything, Eba."

My father used to lecture me on how to become a responsible man one day when I grew up and got married. He was already preparing me, even as young as I was. I wasn't certain whether my relationship with Elena was going to work out in the long run, or whether it would end up as a normal routine for the rest of my life even if I was going to spend it with Elena. After questioning myself I decided to ignore the man who lived inside my head, my inner voice, and reprimanded him, "Stop thinking about all those stupid things, live for today and let tomorrow take care of its own problems."

A wise old man once said, "Too many questions, but there is only one answer." The answer to the questions I asked myself were too far away to be found.

After a year of our unofficial living together, Elena's mother became more involved in our daily lives. She took care of me as if I were her own son. She used to tell me, "Finally we have a man and a son in this family."

One night, Elena woke me up from my sleep and told me the story of her father. She said he had left when she was only three months old and had never come back.

"My mother told me they had argued over child support, and she demanded his full commitment to his responsibilities as a father. My father got angry, as he always did when he was under the influence of alcohol. After a terrible row, my father packed some of his belongings in a backpack along with his documents and left us."

"Did you ever hear from him?" I asked.

"No, never. I grew up seeing my father's clothes still hanging inside his old closet. I often wondered how he smelt and what kind of perfume he wore. Sometimes I go through the pictures he took with my mother when they were in love. I can see something of him in me when I smile in front of a mirror. But I could never figure out what kind of man he really was. My mother didn't tell me much about him, I only hear rumours from some of his old friends about where he could have been living".

As Elena told me her father's story, I felt even more responsible for her as the new man, and perhaps even a father figure, in her life. Elena's family, apart from her mother, was something she kept personal. When I first met Elena, she hadn't talked to me about her family and had never mentioned having any uncles or aunts, or any other extended family. But I did tell her many things about my extended family.

Indeed I come from a culture where extended families are

more important than nuclear families. I told her about how my uncle had raised me and had the right to act as if he was my biological father, and even more.

The time I spent with the Islakers during the early period of our relationship gave me the feeling that I had met my new family. A feeling which built my confidence in trusting people again. I felt like I'd come a rough and long way, from the position of an unpaid butler in my uncle's house to a minor who fell into the wicked hands of people like Samir El Sheik and Sam Moelener. Since Elena had told me the story of her father I experienced a further promotion as I promoted myself to the position of the defender, standing up for someone who had stood up for me at the lowest point of my downfall. I officially named myself chief bodyguard of the Islaker family, a role I would play for as long as I still breathed in oxygen and breathed out gas.

There had been a huge thunderstorm during the day, which was followed by a pitch dark and cold winter evening. Elena and I were relaxing on the sofa in our living room, watching television and having some quality time under the blanket which had saved us from the terrible times. The large blanket, handmade by Elena, was knitted in maroon wool and had an attractive white border.

The television screen was showing a commercial for Barack Obama's speech at Nelson Mandela's 100th international day, which was due to take place the following week. We were waiting to watch the eight o'clock news which would follow the commercial break. Elena was going through her work schedule in her diary while the two cups of tea I had prepared were still too hot for us to drink. After the long commercial break, the main news broke in.

"There was a bombing incident just moments ago. The explosion took place at the central train station in the city."

The news reporter looked wet and cold, rubbing his shivering hands together as he stood outside the train station.

"It has been confirmed that eight people died in the incident and that many others have been taken to hospitals around the city with serious injuries. Some remain in a critical condition." The reporter's flow was interrupted by the newsreader at the main studio. She was a slim woman wearing a thick red blazer with a black shirt underneath. She coughed lightly and then came up with a new development on the story.

"It has now been confirmed by the authorities that the incident at central station was a terrorist attack. According to the police, two suspects were involved in the attack. One of the suspects blew himself up with a wired explosive vest after being shot multiple times by the police. The second suspect, who is believed to have been waiting in a blue mini-bus for the perpetrator, drove off at speedily after he had been spotted by the police. The man is still on the run and police are looking for him."

The reporter on the ground at the station continued with more details on the story as they unfolded. After a few minutes, the studio newsreader broke in again.

"The police have now confirmed the name of the fleeing suspect. His name is Samir El Sheik and he is a citizen of the abandoned city. Samir is believed to have lived as an illegal alien here in the Promised Land a few years ago. If anyone knows the suspect on the run, Samir El Sheik, please report immediately to the nearest police station. The Internal Affairs ministry have put in place a generous reward for anyone who cooperates." The report ended with a picture of Samir, smoking a cigarette, in the corner of the television screen.

I was traumatised by the news, and from seeing the picture of Samir's face. It felt like the face of the long-gone devil I used to know was back. I was seeing the face of the devil, who I believed had long been cast out of this life and would never come back, not in my imagination or my nightmares but in real life.

I thought Samir had died in the boat accident. Even when Doctor Islaker senior told me I was one of two survivors, it had not even crossed my mind that the second survivor could have been Samir. In dismay, I turned my whole body towards Elena with my mouth wide open.

"What's the matter with you?" she asked, her blue eyes widely opened with their shiny lenses penetrating straight into mine. I gave her a confused smile before I responded.

"Nothing love, the news is just shocking to watch."

My mind was racing as I left Elena sitting on the sofa alone and walked out to the balcony.

Standing at the edge of the balcony, I saw two options. One was to throw myself over because I was petrified by seeing Samir's image again, or terrified of seeing him in the flesh. My second option was to run away. But confessing to Elena what I knew about the saga yet not going to the police was a major concern to my conscience. And on the other hand, the idea of not telling Elena the truth about everything filled me with guilt. I quickly decided that if I didn't pull myself together and go down to the police station to tell them everything I knew about Samir, I would be punished by my own conscience for the rest of my life. I also thought there was a risk that if I did not give the authorities the information I had about Samir it could work against me, in my conscience and even by the law which could perceive me as a perpetrator in disguise. After a moment of thinking, I gave myself a second chance to rethink carefully about what decision I should make. I opened my eyes wide and looked up into the sky, thinking deep thoughts that helped me to regain my self-consciousness. I decided to grab the hot pot with my bare hands.

I returned to the living room and said to Elena, "I know that man on the news, the suspect who is on the run."

"You don't mean what you are saying, Eba," Elena replied with dismay.

"Yes, I am sure of it. He is Samir, the desert man, the one I told you about." She stared at me with a frown, as if she was checking whether she could detect guilt in my voice.

"I thought he was killed in the boat accident," I continued, "I didn't know that he had been rescued. Even when your mother told me there was a second survivor, I didn't imagine it could be him." Tears started folding in my eyes, tears which I tried to hold back but couldn't, and streamed down my cheeks.

"I should contact my mother and ask her about this Samir thing." Elena looked devastated as she went to call her mother. I assumed she was thinking that perhaps I knew more about Samir and his network than I had told her. The bombing incident had turned into something personal between me and the fleeing suspect, who had been described on television as dangerous and deadly. A man who was once a friend of mine had now become the greatest foe of not only me, but of a whole nation.

When Elena returned from the phone, she interrupted my thoughts. I was thinking about being thrown out of the walls of the Promised Land again after a year of normal life, and whether what had happened was going to bring a new setback in my life and in my relationship with the woman I cherished so much.

"I have just spoken to my mother. She said it was him, the man on the television is Samir El Sheik. She has confirmed it after crosschecking their old medical records. So, you are right, Eba. Mother told me he was rescued while he was swimming towards the shore. He was extremely weak so he was hastily taken away to the clinic while you were still lying unconscious on the ship."

"Why does it always have to be me?" I asked over and over again.

Elena cuddled me in her arms which gave me courage. We listened calmly while the news report on the television continued. Elena then asked me to turn myself in to the police. It was a difficult decision to make at that moment, but I felt I had no other choice but to do so.

Even though the computer had rejected my story when I arrived in the Promised Land three years earlier, once again I had an opportunity to prove everything I'd told them already. I knew I had to do it, not only for the victims of the attack, but also for myself and for the many other people who Samir and his network may have taken advantage of.

"Would you like me to come with you?" Elena offered.

I accepted gratefully and we left immediately for the police station.

It was busy downtown as we drove to the police station. We saw people laying flowers and lighting candles at the scene where the bombing had taken place, in solidarity and respect for the dead and the injured. Some people stood were holding placards with messages to promote love instead of hate. I saw one woman with a placard which said, 'No one is illegal in this world, set the so-called illegal aliens free!' The words on that woman's placard brought me courage and pride. My mind had been intoxicated for the past three years by the label her placard denounced. People who had unfortunately found themselves in a situation like mine had been labelled as illegal aliens and vagabonds.

'Central Police Station' announced the sign painted in bold white letters on a blue background, installed at the front entrance of the modern three-storey building which had more glass walls than concrete ones. Two special agents, dressed in full operational kits with bulletproof vests and heavy rifles, stood alert and on guard at the main entrance.

The police agent at the counter seemed impatient as she invited us hastily to take a seat in the main office. She looked alarmed when Elena introduced us as partners and told her that I was there as a witness relating to the bombing incident at the central station. My body started shaking and I could hear the metal chair I was sitting on vibrating against the floor.

"Calm down young man," the agent said, "This is a very high-profile case and I want you to know how heroic you are having the courage to come to us. You set a good example."

Inside the anti-terror unit, five seated police agents worked busily behind their desks. The room was polluted by the smell of strong aromatic coffee and I suspected that some secret smoking was going on from the smell which lingered in the air. The situation rapidly became more official and I was scared when the leading detective, a sergeant, thanked Elena for her cooperation and asked her to leave the building with an offer of a ride home.

Elena protested, "I have to stay here with Eba."

"Mam, thank you for your cooperation but I have to insist that you leave the station right now," barked a big bodyguard who had appeared from nowhere and tapped my girlfriend on her back. As he forced her to the main door, Elena continued to resist. She didn't want to leave and I could see a woman who was ready to give her life for her soulmate. The scene in the anti-terror unit was humiliating. Elena and I were separated for the first time since our union and I heard the engine of Elena's car as she drove off.

After Elena had left the station, a physically fit and well-dressed police agent came in wearing a holster containing a black pistol and a long stick. Behind his back I could see some silver handcuffs. His outfit made him look like a super-cop as he accompanied me to the interrogation room. When I raised my head to get a better view of his square face I saw he was wearing dark sunglasses which struck me as strange given we were inside a building on an already dark winter night.

"This is no summertime," I muttered under my breath. I put up a little resistance as the officer started pushing me through the hallway to the interrogation room.

"Why do you have to push me?"

"You have the to remain calm, sir," he answered. His voice sounded heavy and cold like those on my father's old radio when he turned it on.

The sign on the door read 'Interrogation' and it was open, but I couldn't see anyone inside the room as the big agent pushed me into it. I steadily turned around and scanned the room. There was a desk painted in grey and two easy chairs of the same colour facing each other from either side of the desk. The walls were painted plain white and a bright light hung from the ceiling. There were two amplified power speakers installed on the longer walls.

"You have to wait here," the agent in the sunglasses said as he closed the door. I was once again sealed inside a room without a window. The room seemed to be soundproof as I couldn't hear any sound from outside. The atmosphere re-minded me of the room where I was locked up in Samir's house. I was afraid of being abused again, like I had been before, but I tried to calm myself down. After a few minutes, the door was opened again and another man came in. He was smartly dressed in a black striped suit with a small pa-per file which he carried in his right hand. He took the seat opposite of me and started leafing through the papers in his file before he introduced himself.

"Mister Yoko, my name is Inspector Toure. I am repre-senting the anti-terror unit of this police department. I am here to ask you some questions regarding the bombing and terror attack which occurred a few hours ago." He paused and stared at me before continuing. "It will be in the best interests of the law and the people of this land if you coop-erate with us. This establishment will provide you with full witness protection according to law." I felt intimated by his stare, it was clear he was trying to figure out whether I was telling the truth or not. In my tradition it is considered rude to look someone straight in the face, and I still find it difficult to do so. Elena was the first person I had ever looked straight in the eyes. My voice was shaking as I started to explain. The little tape recorder which Toure had laid on the desk kept running slowly on two wheels wrapped with a small brown tape. It looked like a car stuck on a muddy field in the middle of a safari. The thirty minutes interrogation was earnest as Inspector Toure grilled me into grains with critical questions. He was a tall and handsome man who looked like a seasoned policeman with ambitions to climb the ladder of promotion as far as his career was concerned. The ongoing terrorist investigation was a high-profile case designated to him as chief investigator, which made me think it was an opportunity for him to get a one-way ticket all the way to the top of the ranks. The investigator kept on bulldozing me with direct questions, some of which were extremely personal. The pressure he applied to persuade me to talk more made me break into tears several times during the interrogation. At one point Toure took a pouch of cigars from the inner pocket of his jacket. He opened the pouch and picked up a stick of cigar which, having lit with a silver coloured metal lighter, he took few drags of, puffing out the smoke through his nose into the air, before putting it out. He made notes in his small book while he posed his questions to me. During the interrogation, I told him every detail about the agony Samir and his network had put me through. My zeal was uplifted as the interview proceeded, which helped me to break through the barriers of shyness and mistrust which prevented me from telling people the details about what happened between Samir and me. By the end, I felt like I was being reborn as a free bird. 'This is reincarnation!' I shouted in my mind.

When Inspector Toure left, closing the door behind him, the fresh air in the room was overcome by a strong tobacco odour. A few minutes later, the door reopened and a man and woman entered. The woman was carrying an extra folding chair which she sat on and introduced herself as Agent Ranger Miller, representing the Promised Land's border control department. The man introduced himself as Correction Officer Landford, representing the maximum prison department. Miller briefed me about what was going to happen to me.

"Mr Eba Yoko," she said, pronouncing my name badly. "You are a potential witness to a serious ongoing investigation. But in the meantime, you are under arrest for roaming the streets of the Promised Land. You have violated all the rules by floating in and out of the walls illegally." She smiled and winked her eye at me. She wasn't an attractive woman but looked like a tough border guard. I was shocked by Agent Miller's statement which suggested they were planning to put me behind bars for a very long time. Only moments earlier Inspector Toure had promised me witness protection by law if I cooperated, but now I was being told I was going to prison. I was shocked when Correction Officer Landford twisted my hands behind my back and cuffed them up.

Upon our arrival at the maximum-security prison, the inmates cheered us. They chanted, "Fresh meat in the market!" I was taken and locked up in a cell where I met a man who seemed, from his appearance, to have served some length of time inside.

One of the escort guards said, "This is your room, Mr Yoko. Meet your cellmate. You better behave yourself very well."

I threw my blanket on the upper bunk of the metal bunk bed, as its lower one was already occupied by my cellmate. The cell was an eight foot square room, unpainted but coloured by the normal baked bricks which made up its walls. The toilet seat was uncovered, and it smelt like waste from boiled eggs.

The man lying on the lower bunk was covered with a green blanket and, before I had settled into the cell, he began coughing and cursing in a low tone. When my cellmate coughed he sounded like a very old and sick man, but he was about the same age as my father I guessed. After I'd been in our cell a few minutes, he stood up and offered me his hand warmly. His friendly greeting was hospitable which put me at ease.

"Don't be scared of this place, son. My name is Professor Shuber," he introduced himself.

"I am Eba Yoko."

"You must have come from far away from here I guess, Eba?"

"Yes, you are right, I came from the other side of the ocean."

"Oh, I understand, the Continent of the Lions it must be. If that is so, I have been there a couple of times before when I was stronger. But life is not fair, son," Shuber uttered and shook his head, and he asked me to take some rest.

When I awoke from a short nap, I noticed that my cellmate was sitting up quietly on his bed, engrossed in the book he was reading.

"Oh, you are up," he said when he noticed that I was awake.

"They will let us go outside soon and we can have some fresh air."

"Thank you, sir."

"Never mind, just call me Shuber," he declared.

"What brought you here, son?"

"I don't know exactly," I avoided the truth, it was too early for me to tell him my story about Samir and the rest.

"Yes, son," he said, "sometimes the winds of injustice sweep away the innocent ones. I think life is like a tornado, it doesn't choose where to hit. Shuber began telling me his life story.

"I was twenty-four years of age when I graduated from a college of science and technology. After that I quickly found myself a job and a few months later I got married to my girl-friend, the most beautiful woman in the world. A woman that loved me. Oh yes, she loved me so much I considered myself a lucky man. But let me tell you something, after a year of sweet married life I started messing up, and I screwed everything up with my alcohol problem at the time."

Shuber couldn't deviate from telling me the whole truth about himself as he continued.

"I didn't see my daughter grow up. I only heard from old friends of mine that she is now a fully-grown woman and a medical doctor just like her mother," he paused and looked up at the ceiling, nodding. I saw he had shed a few tears and, at that moment, my mind ran directly to the Islakers.

Shuber's story had started to match a picture I had seen before. I had heard a story of a father and husband who had left and never returned. As I was mulling things over in my mind, Professor Shuber interrupted my thoughts and continued to tell me his story.

"My life was turned upside down, and became even worse when I left my wife and my little baby girl. I end up in here due to a conspiracy with a murder case. It was the other woman I was in love with. She was also addicted to drugs and alcohol."

I was curious and decided to ask him a few questions.

"What are the names of your wife and daughter?"

He looked at me with his pale blue eyes and answered.

"Elena is the name of my little one, and Marion Islaker used to be my wife." He bowed his head in shame. I could see a round bald patch in the middle of his head, surrounded by hair which had mostly turned grey.

My mouth was shaking as I tried to restrain my lips from telling him what I knew of the names he had mentioned. I wanted to tell him how much pain he left them with, how Elena misses him. But my second thought told me not to say a word. There was no doubt in my mind that Professor Shuber was Elena's father. Without saying anything more to him, I rested my cheek back on the pillow and closed my eyes. I kept on thinking about my loved one, Elena, the woman who chose to be with me only because of who I am.

The next morning, while I was busy with my push-ups in our cell to keep fit, two prison guards appeared in front of the door and informed me that a visitor was waiting to see me. I knew straight away that the visitor would be Elena. I saw her through the thick soundproof glass inside the visiting room. She looked frustrated and exhausted. She gave me a twisted smile and picked up the telephone on her side of the glass.

"I have arranged a lawyer who can defend you, and also help us win the right to stay together as partners legally. It means I must take full responsibility for you until you are able to find a legally paid job. But there is a problem." She bowed her head, as if she was shy about what she had to tell me.

"What is the problem?"

"The rules say we must have known each other for two years before we could start any process to get married, and we only met a year ago. That is the reason why the computer rejected my request. Stupid rules." I could see that her heart was broken, she was filled with so much pain that hot tears ran down her reddened cheeks. We sat in silence and looked at each other through the glass.

"You have one minute left," the timekeeper announced. Elena stood and put her lips to the glass to kiss me before she left.

Back in my cell, I kept thinking about the lessons my late friend Yalla Banke had taught me before he passed away. He left me with nothing but a good piece of advice. I started asking myself deep questions, such as why do people stereotype others who are also a part of the ship that carries the human race? Yalla once said to me, "If your neighbour goes to bed hungry and then suspects the next morning that you are throwing food in your dustbin, that neighbour would try by any means to pay you a kind visit even if he is not welcomed or invited by you."

Inside the walls of the Promised Land, I observed that people were throwing a lot of good things in the dustbin, things that could be useful to many people in other parts of the world. Giving unwanted but useful goods to others who are in need can be a great purpose in life and an opportunity to make others feel better. Inside the walls, I often came across dustbins filled with food that was wasted despite much of it still being fresh. People wasted a lot, while other people were fighting among themselves for food on the other side of the walls. Sometimes I thought it wasn't worth living in this world, a world filled with prejudice, hatred and confusion. I even reached the conclusion that my friend Yalla Banke had decided to take his own life because of the disappointments he suffered throughout his entire life. On the other hand, whenever I thought about Elena and the little things which made us so happy I told myself that it was a blessing to be loved, healthy and wake up every morning to find out that you are still alive. My thoughts kept me busy and took me to another world, as I kept on asking myself questions. But the good thing was I always ended up encouraging myself with the one thing I believed, something I couldn't see, which was called hope with some amount of reality.

It was already late in the night when Shuber woke me up from my sleep and asked me to lend him my ears for a moment.

"There is something I would like to share with you. I know for sure that both of us are going to be set free today, it will happen just after the sun comes up. But I want you to do me a favour. I know that my daughter is still alive and living inside the walls of the Promised Land and I want you to deliver this envelope to her, it contains a letter." Shuber sounded like someone who was going to go off on their travels with no hope of returning.

"Eba," he said, "I am going to be free and so are you. If you find my daughter, make sure she reads this letter. Since I left them I never wanted to let them see my face again as my soul is weighed down with guilt and shame." He let out a loud cry before he continued.

"Eba, people think that men don't cry, but I want you to know this, if someone says to you that men don't cry, tell that person it is a lie, because real men do cry."

"That's right, Shuber," I agreed.

The belief that men shouldn't cry was set in concrete in my tradition. I had only once seen my father crying, in an isolated corner behind our garden where he thought no one could see him. That was the day his mother passed away. My father was probably shy about crying in front of his friends and family, as when I reflect back to that day it is clear he had a good reason to even cry without being ashamed.

I took the white envelope from Shuber and said to him, "I will make sure I deliver this letter to your daughter and take good care of her if she would allow me. I promise you."

Shuber smiled, his face visibly relaxing, and thanked me for my promise. Since the first day I met him in the prison cell when he told me his story, I had known that he was the father of the woman I was in love with. But being in love with his daughter Elena was a truth which I had never disclosed to him, I hadn't even told him that I knew her mother, his wife.

"Eba Yoko!" called a strong male voice as the steel door of our cell creaked and was unlocked by two big prison guards. They came in and asked me to follow them outside because I was free. It was dawn already but I wasn't fully awake, and Shuber was still sleeping. I hurriedly put on my own clothes which the prison guards had brought in with them. By the time I finished dressing, the guards were busy checking on my cellmate who still hadn't stirred from his sleep. The guards were suddenly silent and I saw them exchange a strange look, which made me take a better look at how they had checked on Shuber so closely without waking him. I saw the white saliva which came from his mouth, overflowing as it ran down Shuber's chin and wetting his orange inmate overalls.

"He is gone," said one of the guards, "call the medics."

Professor Shuber was declared dead. The confirmation of his death was like another piercing arrow through my heart, especially because of my deep connection with his own daughter.

I realised that this was the freedom which he had foreseen the night before, a true prophecy.

At least we were both freed, just as he had told me we would be. That was the final chapter of Shuber's book. "Rest in peace my friend," I whispered hoarsely.

I stood still, closed my eyes and said a prayer as the medics lifted the old man's stiffened corpse out of the room.

I was then summoned to face the prison warden in his office which was located in the tallest tower of the prison. The height of the tower gave me the opportunity to have a complete view of the cage in which I was locked up. I was amused while climbing the narrow stairway that led to the head of the prison's office, because the two guards who accompanied me struggled for breath and panted as they climbed the stairs.

I trembled as I entered the office, which was overflowing with untidy brown files and had a broad L-shaped wooden desk against the north wall of the room. The director sat on a leather swivel chair with his face turned to the wall and his back to me. He was silent for about thirty seconds before he twisted the 360-degree moving chair round and I saw his face. A tall and ugly looking figure with a long chin, which gave him a strange facial appearance but the expression of a true disciplinarian.

"My name is Max Mc Koi, director of this facility," he began twisting his untamed moustache as he spoke proudly.

"Mr Yoko, you are being released based on the facts that you gave in a testimony, which to us is worth more than any other treasure you can think about in human history. The testimony you gave and the things you told us about Samir El Sheik and his gang have all been verified by the anti-terror unit. Your description of places, and the names of people that you mentioned in the interrogation room, is information which has paved the way to a successful start of the primary investigation."

He paused for a few moments as he made himself a cup of coffee. He mimed the words to a song that could be heard faintly from a radio in a nearby office while he waited for the coffee machine to signal that his drink was ready. He resumed addressing me while sipping his coffee.

"A coffee for one," he said jubilantly, "inmates don't share the same coffee pot with guards Mr Yoko." He repositioned himself in the chair and took another sip of coffee before continuing.

"For your information, Samir and his network were tracked down and arrested as a direct result of the information you shared. They have been indicted to face a judge so they will be tried and judged according to international law. We believe we have broken the backbone of Samir and his devilish network, which will soon be demolished." He opened a blue file and began signing its pages. "Sign here," he said, "you are free to go, but one more thing before you leave. The King of the Promised Land has granted you a permit to stay here legally and permanently. Your problems are over, Eba." I signed the various papers Mc Koi handed to me and took my leave through the door by which I had entered.

After Mc Koi had officially ordered my release, I stepped out of the main prison gate to find two police officers leaning on a white patrol vehicle, waiting to accompany me back to Elena's apartment as a free man. But when I arrived home, Elena and I struggled to find peace. We were weak and tired and spent a lot of time just hanging around the apartment watching the news about Samir and his gang. The news reports confirmed that they had been apprehended due to the testimony of an unnamed illegal alien, who had himself been a victim in many waves of abuse by Samir and his network. The news also announced that the unnamed alien had agreed to appear as a witness in the case against Samir El Sheik in the magistrates court of human rights and criminal justice, with the first proceedings due to commence soon.

The news reporters described me like a little masked hero who nobody knew the identity of. Even though I was determined to take Samir and his gang on in court, I wasn't pleased that I was being portrayed as a hero. My expectation had been that the authorities would have protected me and not even mentioned that there was a witness. The ongoing news coverage about the story made me feel vulnerable, and was a distraction to my personal life. I could see from the way Elena looked that she was hopeful, but also tired and insecure. In the kitchen, I looked at Elena gave her a big hug, and said, "Thank you, for everything."

"You don't have to thank me, I did it for us. I should thank you."

I was worried about explaining the news of her father's tragedy to Elena. There was a witness protection officer from the protection unit deployed in our apartment in case of any threat. We needed him there, but it was awkward when I realised I couldn't prevent him from hearing Elena crying after she read the letter from her father. But I couldn't bear to hold it any longer.

Sitting on the couch next to Elena, I called her attention with a trembling voice,

"Elena, I met a man with whom I shared a cell in prison."

She then focused all of her attention on me and listened attentively.

"The man was also from the Promised Land and he gave me something to deliver to someone."

I went into the bedroom and returned with the envelope, which I handed to her.

"Here," I said, "open it, you might have an idea about where it has come from."

When Elena finished reading, she dropped the note unconsciously and stared with wide eyes towards the balcony. I knew right away that the bigger story had just been broken, a story which will be difficult to tell even to Elena's next generation and one that will forever devastate her whenever she thinks about it. Worried about what she would do next, I reached for Elena in an attempt to comfort her with a hug, but she pushed me away and looked up to the ceiling. like a burning candle, tears streamed down her face. She lowers her head and looked me in the face again nodded with a gesture of disappointment and walked away. Doctor Islaker senior arrived for a tea-drinking appointment we had arranged a few days earlier. I explained to her what was going on in the house, Dr Islaker senior picked up the letter written by the hand of her ex-husband and read it. Although she appeared shocked by the letter from Shuber, it seemed as if she somehow already knew that her husband's life would end miserably. She handed the letter to me as if inviting me to read it, which I did. It was short.

Dear Marion and Elena,

I am writing to express my love and gratitude to you both.
I am aware of how much pain and disappointment I have caused in your lives. As I am writing I am in prison, where I will spend the rest of my days. In this note, I want to ask you both to forgive me for all the cruelty I have inflicted on you.
I don't have the words to describe my dejected life and I am now locked up for good and forever because of the poor choices I made.
I know for sure we will be reunited in the life after. I will go ahead and prepare a home for us on the other side of the river. I will prepare a home where we can do all the things we've missed doing together as family. I will prepare a home where we will stay warm together as a family, for eternity.
Take good care of yourselves.

Your love, Shuber Mathius.

There were murmurings and small meetings going on inside the crown court number one as the audience waited for the chief judge to appear. My stomach was burning like I had a piece of paper on fire inside me as I sat, next to my lawyers, near the court clerk. I could see people sceptically pointing their fingers at me as if to indicate to their friends or acquaintances that I was the one. The press presence was immense as reporters from newspapers and the electronic media geared themselves up to pick the bones out of the flesh. At the media booth a woman was busily drawing, and as she looked at me keenly every five seconds I assumed she was drawing a portrait of me.

My spirits were lifted slightly when my eyes met with Elena's from where she sat, together with her mother, amongst the general audience. She smiled at me and winked. I winked back and managed a forced smile before returning to my nervous state.

"Don't worry, Eba. We are going to nail them right away," said Jaal Brown, the leading attorney on my legal team.

I was baffled as I hadn't heard that phrase used before and had no idea what he meant by it. I concluded it must mean that if Samir and his gang were found guilty they would be sentenced to death by hanging.

"All rise!" the bailiff ordered. He stood up straight like a soldier on guard of honour or in a parade. Everyone stood up in respect of the court order and of the chief judge. A man of pensionable age emerged. He was dressed in a red full-bottomed robe with a black scarf hanging around his neck. His short bench horsehair wig, curled and grey, was steady and shining.

Judge J. S. Sommerset, according to the name tag placed on the front of his desk, appeared in the room with his full team of seven men who made up the jury. They took their various positions in the courtroom.

"The court may sit," the judge invited, having already taken his seat and started leafing through a large file in front of him. The jurors took their seats in the jury box, a separate space bordered by a low fence of highly-polished wood.

"Call the case the State versus Samir El Sheik, George Gleen and Karamokoh Dambay." Judge Sommerset began presiding on the case. He looked at the audience, his eyes lowered slightly under his thick glasses.

A door close to the juror's box opened, and a well-built, no-nonsense prison guard came into the courtroom, closely followed by the three accused men who appeared in orange overalls with their hands in cuffs. The prison guard uncuffed them and stepped aside, but not too far away from them. I was shocked to see Karamokoh with the other accused as they stood inside the prosecution box. I hadn't been informed that he was one of those on trial, neither had I heard from him in all those years. I was angry with the authorities who I felt should have informed me earlier about the details of the case, or at least told me the names of all the people standing trial.

Karamokoh's face looked dark, bitter and unshaved as he entered the dock, as did those of Samir and George who appeared behind him. They didn't see that I was in the room before they took their seats. They gazed directly at the judge with pitiful eyes as they sat down.

The court settled into perfect decorum as the bench clerk, a short man dressed in a tight-fitting blue suit, began to read out the charges.

"First accused Samir El Sheik, charged with terrorism, human trafficking, sexual abuse of male and female minors and money laundering by the state of the Promised Land according to international law. Samir El Sheik will face his honour, the Chief Judge of the Crown Court of the State, and will have the right to defend himself against the above-mentioned charges according to law. No one is guilty of accusations made until he or she is found wanting through a legal process in a court of law." The bench clerk diligently repeated a similar statement for the other two, who were each charged with human trafficking and money laundering, before bowing his head to the judge and taking his seat.

The judge asked the three accused whether they were guilty of the charges levied against them by the state as they had been read. They all pleaded not guilty to all the accusations and there was another wave of murmuring across the room.

"Order in the court!" the bailiff yelled.

Silence in the courtroom was restored and the state plaintiff was asked by the judge to make his case. I waited anxiously for Mr Lombardo De Browne, a sharp and experienced state prosecutor in his middle age, to begin his case. He confidently grilled the three men into grains, using the evidence and proof he had gathered from the testimony I had given.

To my surprise, Mr Lombardo even produced a copy of the letter which Samir's heartbroken wife had written and left with me to deliver on her behalf to her husband at their house in the abandoned city.

"Your honour," the prosecutor addressed the judge, "this is a letter I found myself inside a tiny room where I believe my witness here was locked up at the premises of Mr Samir El Sheik. This piece of evidence, along with many others, was recovered during a joint crack down operation with the police in various locations."

Lombardo also produced photographed skeletons left behind by the remains of the men murdered at Samir's house when I was held hostage, by the men who spared my life only because I had to deliver their message to Samir.

A wealth of tangible evidence was produced in front of the judge by the prosecutor, including data showing mobile telecommunication exchanges between Samir, Karamokoh and George. Some of their telephone exchanges had been wiretapped and the audio recordings were played in front of the court. Substantial amounts of cash in foreign currencies was found in the possession of Karamokoh and George, which they were unable to provide a proper account of. The list of evidence went on and on. I was impressed by Mr Lombardo's performance. He had clearly prepared the case well with sufficient evidence to enable my lawyers to have an easy time in court. They just sat next to me, relaxed as if they were just listeners in a courtroom somewhere during a winter vacation. My lawyers had little to add to the proceedings as it seemed like the hard meat was already being grilled to grains by the prosecutor.

"Your honour," Lombardo continued, "these three men standing in front of you, according to my findings, are the sorts of evil characters who prevent people sleeping soundly at night. These men are cankerworms to our civilised society. Lombardo paused and pulled a white handkerchief from his pocket which he used to wipe his sweaty face.

"Your honour, these men are nothing more than common criminals. I believe it is just a matter of time before we witness their pathetic downfall, and that of their organisation."

Lombardo rested his case and retreated to his seat next to the jury.

Judge J.S. Sommerset asked me to take the seat in the witness box as the court had questions which I could help provide answers to. Samir and his friends seemed shocked as they watched me take an oath of affirmation.

The three accused men, who had spent their lives believing they were the strongest of all, raised their heads in a stunned silence as their bodies visibly tensed. I could see Samir's chest expand as if he wanted to attack someone. I knew first-hand how Samir reacted when he was in shock or furious. The three of them looked at me like a little animal they wanted to skin alive and eat raw. They were well aware that I was an authentic witness to their crimes. A witness who had the means to bend them down onto their knees and watch them rot in prison for the rest of their wicked lives.

"I, Eba Yoko," I repeated the oath after the court clerk, "solemnly and sincerely swear that everything I say in this court will be the truth, and nothing but the truth, so help me God."

After being sworn under oath, I told the court everything I knew of the three accused men and about all the things Samir had put me through. When I had finished giving my evidence I felt like the strongest man ever. I felt strong to have faced the men who once ruined my life. They thought I was weak, but there I was in a courtroom showing them that I was the stronger of us. One of the defence lawyers began bombarding me with questions. Some of them were critical and offensive and I found them difficult, and pain-

ful, to answer. The defendant's lawyers were mean to me, to
the extent that one of them referred to me as a liar. It made
me sore and, feeling humiliated, I started answering their
questions in a more brutal manner. My anger started to
get the better of me and weakened me. I could tell that my
own monster was about to turn against me. My anger gave a
small advantage to the desperate and ambitious young defence lawyer who voluntarily took the case to defend Samir
and his allies. I was angry because someone was trying to
degrade me in front of a crown court during the proceedings of a high federal case. Samir's defence lawyers wanted
to turn the truth around, in the name of the law, by accus-
ing me of telling lies about the criminals in the dock. The
defence lawyer was unrelenting with his false accusations
against me, even after the judge had warned him. He had
discovered my weaker side which he exploited as he continued mocking me through his questioning. He told the judge
that I was not telling the truth, despite being under oath,
and that he doubted whether I had ever met any of the three
accused before the case.

I realised later that I had been inexperienced and too
naïve to understand how the legal system worked, and that
I'd climbed up to the highest degree of stupidity by trying to
prove my honesty by exercising my anger in front of a judge.

"Mr Sandowsky," one of my lawyers interrupted the defence lawyer with a firm voice and objected. "Stop pushing
my client, a potential witness representing the people, into
the corner. It is constitutionally wrong to obstruct justice,
especially inside a court." Lombardo continued, "This is not
a police investigation any more, this is a court case, I hope
my learned friend here will learn from this day." The audi-

ence in the courtroom broke into a peal of laughter as my lawyer ended his objection, causing the bailiff to call for order. There was order.

"I sustain the witness may proceed," the judge ruled.

"Yes, your honour," Sandowsky admitted and retreated to his defence council.

"Eba Yoko, you may proceed," the judge ordered.

I continued my part of prosecuting the three accused men by telling my story to the court, straight from the depth of my heart. The audience listened in a solemn silence as I told the court about my experience at the hands of Samir and his associates. I told them everything in that courtroom, leaving nothing out, which took me back to my bitter past. Sharing my experiences in front of so many people opened many of the layers of my unhealed wounds, but telling the truth and letting it go also helped in some way to heal my old wounds. I described in raw detail the damage that Samir and his friends had done to me, and also to many other people I met along the way.

When I was done with confessing to the court, the judge asked me only one question.

"Eba Yoko," he said, "Do you know these three accused men?" and pointed his index finger towards Samir, Karamokoh and George.

"Yes, my lord," I answered, without fear or doubt. At that moment I felt like a soldier who had to fight to save his own life, and the lives of many others, in a hostile situation. A nobleman once said, "When you save one life, you save the whole world. When you take one innocent life, you take all the innocent lives in the whole world."

Even though I had refused to become a soldier in arms for

my country in a physical sense I had, through the part I had played in this case, become a soldier in my mind, body and spirit.

The judge hit his desk twice with a small wooden hammer and announced a break.

"At this point, I retire the court to a break. Proceedings will be recessed for thirty minutes," he declared.

My lawyers appeared pleased with my performance inside the witness box and were optimistic about how the trial was progressing. Their proud body language predicted what the outcome of the case might be. My heartbeat raced as the two advocates discussed their tactics for the next court session. I kept a tight hold on the glass of water I was served at my request in the courtroom, but my stomach was far too uneasy for me to take a sip out of it. It was a strange feeling and I couldn't distinguish between excitement and nervousness. During the conversation between my lawyers in the waiting room, we heard popping sounds like someone was making fried corn. My lawyers stopped speaking and listened attentively. We then heard banging on the door from outside and the sound of running footsteps. We were trying to get close to the small window, to observe what was going on outside, when the door of the waiting toom was opened by one of the court's security men who said to us, "We need to get you out of here, there is some misunderstanding outside the court-yard."

My lawyers and I followed the security guard who took us to a group of police officers dressed in full riot kits and holding assault rifles. On our way out, the popping sounds didn't sound the same any longer, they had become louder and clearer and I realised we were hearing gunshots.

The commander of the small unit of riot police briefed us, as bullets were still flying through the air in the court-yard. "Gentlemen, you must stay here with these two men for your own safety. The rest of the team have to go to work."

From the window, where I took cover behind the curtain, I peeped through to see what was going on outside. I saw two gunmen dressed in black, wearing woolly masks with holes for their eyes, taking cover behind a black jeep. I watched as they opened fire against a unit of police officers who were defending the main entrance of the crown court. The two gunmen looked like they had nothing to lose. They fired random shots before retiring from their position behind the jeep and retreating a few metres behind them to a manhole in the street drainage. One of the masked men lifted the thick metal drainage cover, put it aside and squeezed him-self into the manhole. I couldn't believe my eyes as I watched his whole body and his head disappear into the hole, closely followed by his comrade. They made their way down into the tunnel, but they were about to be overrun by the heavy reinforcements from the anti-terror who had arrived to take care of the situation. The troops held their fire and wait-ed for a few minutes before they advanced carefully, with slow and steady steps, towards the black vehicle which the attackers had hidden behind during the gunfire. The way they moved, so precisely, made me think they suspected that the jeep had been wired with a bomb. One officer fired a few close range shots in different directions and one of them hit the jeep. The rest of the officers waited for a moment before one of their teammates, dressed in a white bomb protection suit, confidently made his way towards the vehicle and started examining it.

Where I stood, my pants were wet as I couldn't hold on to my excretion. The men who had studied hard to become lawyers and given their lives to defending the law and constitution were lying flat on the floor. Their heads were pressed against the ground and they didn't dare to raise them even a single inch. I imagined they had never heard a real gunshot before in their lives.

The two attackers were quickly followed into the drain by a small team of police agents, and I desperately hoped they would be apprehended in the sewer. I watched as the mysterious abandoned jeep, which hadn't exploded, was carefully towed away by an engineering unit from the military.

In the immediate calm after the dramatic gunfire I started worrying about Elena. I didn't know where she was or what could have happened to her and her mother during the chaos in the courtyard. I got the news that they were safe from a court correspondent who came into the room and gave us details about the repelled attack at the court.

The court correspondent told us the attack had been confirmed as an act of terror and was an attempt to sabotage the court proceedings in the case. The attackers had attempted to kidnap Samir and the other defendants in some kind of rescue mission.

"The hearing of the case has been postponed indefinitely until you hear from the court," the correspondent explained.

After listening to the court correspondent's briefing, I was terrified. The case was actually becoming bigger and was far from over. I had wanted to be a genuine witness in court, but instead I had been caught in the middle of a state case which was rapidly escalating into extreme violence.

I could already smell the media heat. I knew that the siege at the court would be the main news on every television channel in the Promised Land, and that explosive captions would be plastered across the front page of every newspaper the next morning. After a few hours, I was reunited with Elena who was shaking uncontrollably. She was emotionally broken by everything that was happening.

Our witness protection arrangements were beefed up to two heavily-armed men, which helped us to feel a little safer. On the other hand, they had to follow us everywhere we went and listened to our private conversations, even inside the house. They watched us when we kissed, and when we cried. Perhaps even more humiliating was that whenever I went to the toilet they would hear that too, the gurgling sound of the flush, and possibly even smell the odour of my waste.

A month later we were back in courtroom number one. The courtroom was not as full as it had been for the first hearing. Only a few seats were occupied, mainly by people who were carefully selected and seriously concerned. I was informed that Elena, who wanted to be present for the court session, wasn't allowed to attend for security reasons.

During the second hearing, I couldn't see a single person that I recognised among the small audience. I was racked with fear that, despite the intensive security surrounding the court, Samir's friends might decide to pay the court another visit. I thought about the road I'd travelled only to find myself at such a slippery destination, standing before a judge in a court of justice with reporters, bodyguards, defendants and prosecutors all with their attention focused on me in a high-profile case. I knew I had to play a major role in a case which could lead to social justice for me and the people of the Promised Land.

The court resumed again and everyone rose as the judge and his jury entered the courtroom. He looked proud, confident and well-dressed in his ceremonial costume.

The courtroom fell silent as the judge read the charges. He briefed the court with some details regarding the case, and about the unfortunate incident which had delayed the last proceedings for a month. He then said that the jury had reached their verdict, and that he was going to announce it.

"The jury has reached a verdict in the case between the State and Samir El Sheik, Karamokoh Dambay and George Gleen," the judge began and then paused while a wave of murmuring swept through the audience in the courtroom.

"Order! Order!" the bailiff called for calm, and there was order at once.

Judge J. S. Sommerset continued to read the final verdict.

"By the powers invested in me and the jury of this court, I am the sole custodian who is responsible for announcing the court's verdict and I will do so with sincerity and in respect of the laws that govern this land."

The judge lowered his head and raised his eyes, looking directly at the three accused men as he began announcing their respective crimes, charges and punishments.

He started with Samir El Sheik, the number one accused person in the trial, who was found guilty by the jury on all of the charges brought against him.

He was found guilty of terrorism, conspiracy in the murdering of many innocent people on the Mahera sea, sexual abuse, human trafficking and money laundering. He was sentenced to ninety-six years in prison without any form of appeal allowable under any circumstances.

His collaborators, Karamokoh Dambay and George Gleen, were both charged with human trafficking and money laundering. They were each sentenced to seventy years imprisonment with hard labour.

The judge and his team of jurors left the courtroom immediately after the reading of the final verdict.

The three men who had just been officially criminalised and convicted were taken by heavily-armed police officers, while a handful of concerned citizens from the audience came to congratulate me with tight hugs and kisses. I overheard an old woman, who must have been in her late-seventies, say shakily, "What a hero he was, that young fella."

"We won, Eba. You did a great job," my lawyer said excitedly, exposing the fact that he would be able to make ends meet out of the victory. He looked like a trader who had just clinched a double profit. A drip of sweat ran down his bald head and slowly settled on his right temple.

"Thank you, sir," I replied, "but can I ask you a question before you leave Mr Lombardo?"

"Yes sure," he said curiously.

"What did you mean when you said we were going to nail them this time?"

He smiled and replied, "We just did Eba. It means we are going to bring them down on their knees and to justice."

"Good of you for helping me learn, sir."

"Any time, Eba. Here is my card."

We shook hands and went our separate ways.

A few days after the trial, I received a letter inviting me and Elena to dine with the king of the Promised Land and the entire royal family. The invitation, for the following evening, was a huge surprise for me and I struggled to believe that an ordinary person could be invited to dine at the palace. I asked myself why such things were coming to me now and wished they could have come to me the night I went to bed hungry and passed the night in an abandoned building. Most of all I wished it could have all happened when Yalla Banke was still alive.

"Tomorrow we will be special guests inside the royal palace," I told Elena.

My announcement caused her mouth to drop open for a few a seconds and she was momentarily speechless.

After a hesitant pause she asked, "Do we have to go?"

"Yes, we must be there, it is an invitation from the king himself," I said enthusiastically.

I was excited, but Elena didn't seem enthused about the upcoming event, she just sat back and withdrew into her comfort zone.

Her reaction reduced my excitement and I wondered why she thought it wasn't clever of me to accept the invitation at once. I remembered my father had frequently advised me that I should never turn down a humble invitation.

I cuddled her and said, "We could go to the palace tomorrow in honour of his royalty and listen to what he has to say to us".

Elena responded to my words of encouragement. She turned her body fully into my embrace and held her hands around me tightly.

"I am prepared to do that, but I am scared to meet the royals. Sometimes the royal sword has two sharp edges, Eba. You never know which one of them they might turn against you."

At three the next afternoon, Elena and I dressed in smart clothes according to the dress code explained in the invitation letter. I wore a light-brown suit with a white shirt underneath, thanks to Elena's mother who had bought it for me before we attended a theatre and dinner the previous Christmas. My hair was neatly cut and shaped by Leon, a trusted male hairdresser who worked at the hairdressing salon where Doctor Islaker senior's hair was usually treated, and Elena's too.

Elena wore a magnificent purple dress which had twinkling diamond-shaped beads neatly adorning the front. She looked like a flower seed which had shot up from its roots and manifested into a beautiful rose. Her hair was gathered neatly, tied at the back of her neck, underneath a fabulous green felt hat on her head. We held hands as we stepped out towards the royal car which waited in front of our door to take us to the palace, and when we arrived we majestically walked hand in hand towards its giant arrowed front gates. We were accompanied by the driver who was dressed in a black suit and wore white hand gloves.

We followed the direction of a signboard announcing the 'Main Entrance and Reception.' My nervousness intensified as we spotted two guards, dressed in traditional ceremonial red uniforms, standing alert with swords hanging from the armour around their waists.

The guards stood perfectly straight and silent. At the right corner of the main gate there was a small hut made of old stone bricks with a clay roof. The hut was part of the main gate, though had its own separate little entrance.

"They are here on an invitation from his majesty," the driver explained to the receptionist. The baby-faced lady, dressed in old traditional clothing, smiled at us warmly.

"I knew that before you arrived here, Mr Panjan," she responded flatly to the driver before turning to me.

"You must be the hero from the Continent of the Lions. I've heard so much about you on the radio." She turned again to the driver and said, "As for you, Mr Panjan, you have been summoned to go immediately and pick up young Princess Mary from the summer palace." The baby-faced lady sounded like she was very familiar with the royals and had served them for a long time, as she seemed to know a lot about them.

The baby-faced lady coached us on how to behave in front of the royals.

"When you greet the king make sure you address him as your majesty, and you must bow your head down." She paused and smiled at us again before continuing to educate us on how to behave in front of the royals.

"You are not allowed to sit down until the king has taken his seat. You must not use any kind of street language, or say too much to the king at the dining table. You must wait until the king had tasted his food before you start yours. When you are leaving the king, you must take three steps backwards and then bow before you turn around. Welcome to the royal palace."

She handed us a map of the palace and we were accompanied by one of the king's main guards who had arrived as we were being coached.

The palace was fenced by a great wall built with solid iron rocks. Its surroundings were beautiful, a touch of magic from the hands of mother nature. The fallen leaves from the trees formed into heaps which exaggerated the beautiful autumnal colours of green, red and yellow. The palace stood in the middle of vast grounds and was surrounded by tall trees which were inhabited by colourful rainbow lorikeet parrots. We could see the elegant birds as they jiggled from one tree to another, pecking the wood and preening each other's feathers.

We passed through a long hallway, warmly decorated with paintings glittering in gilt frames, on a deep red carpet. We finally arrived at the great hall where the king and his household stood, in their royal attire, waiting to receive us. I observed from a distance that few of the royals were smiling. It was a long room with a rectangular ceiling which was decorated with different artwork made of gold and there were gigantic lights hanging from the wooden braces of the roof. The windows in the hall were vast, allowing the natural light to stream in through their colourful glass which made the hall even brighter. The floor was covered with light-brown marble tiles and was decorated with a series of small Persian carpets.

The king and queen welcomed us, together with the rest of the household, and we bowed in front of them as we had been instructed. We walked together across the tiled dining room to where a beautiful young lady, dressed in a long pink dress, was playing a classical tune on the piano.

"We are delighted to have you join us for dinner. You may sit," The queen granted us permission to take our places on the luxurious dining chairs after the king was already seated on his chair at the centre of the table facing everyone. Servants in white aprons brought food from the kitchen, which was carefully served with pleasant smiles. The enormous dining table was dressed with a luxurious gold and red cloth with silver frills on the edge, and was filled lavishly with a diverse range of food on silver platters.

I was surprised to see a traditional dish from my country, it was the first time I had laid my eyes on it since I left home. The smell of that part of the menu made my mouth wet with saliva.

"You may eat and drink as much as you want. Your names are now written amongst the heroes of our time, Eba and Elena," the king complimented.

"Thank you, Your Majesty," I replied, with my head slightly bowed.

"You are most welcome."

The king was an old man, much older than I had expected him to be. I remembered having heard that he was still young when he was crowned after the death of his mother, the last queen.

"We have the best cooks from all over the world," the king boasted.

"I can tell, Your Majesty."

"Yes, it is an old tradition of ours," the king said, "for us, food is gold and dining is a ritual. My great grandfather ruled his people with the principle of sustainable food production and the values of hygiene in the kitchen. And still to this day we are known across the whole world for being the best wine producers. That is just the tip. The fountains built through the brains of our family are still flowing high even in present days."

When the king mentioned that they have the best wine it reminded me Sam Moelener, who had said that to me when I first arrived in the Dune. The king and I had a fluent exchange about issues regarding culture and tradition. I told him about where I was born, our culture and traditions and all about the mango trees.

Elena was quiet most of the evening, though she did have some discussion with the queen and her two daughters.

"I have a proposal for you, Eba," the king announced. I stopped eating my fufu and sawa-sawa soup which I was close to finishing and paid full attention to what the king was about to propose to me.

"According to the laws of the Promised Land," he said, "you are not allowed to stay as an illegal alien inside the walls. But your act of bravery in combination with the information you gave during your testimony accelerated the biggest investigation in the history of this country. It has given me the audacity to use my power to change your situation in my land. As an expression of my gratitude for what you have done, I am, as you are aware, intending to grant you a royal pardon to stay by the powers invested in me by my people. From this moment on, you will become a citizen of the Promised Land and will have the same rights as Elena or any other citizen of this land."

A wave of silence passed through the table after the king's proposal, as everyone held on to their knives and forks and stared at each other in dismay. The king smiled and everyone smiled back at him, everyone except Elena and me.

I had no doubt that the queen already knew about the king's proposal, as she looked delighted. But Elena didn't, and she just gave me a hard look. In most cases, Elena was very good at communicating with me through her eyes. But in this case it was not about her shiny sky-blue eyes, or what she may have thought about the proposal, it was about me. I had to decide based on what I believed.

After a moment of silence in which I considered what I must say, I looked at the king directly.

"Your Majesty," I said, "With all due respect to you, the queen and the rest of your family I would like to say we are so grateful for your hospitality, for honouring us with this wonderful dinner and, most of all, for your offer for me to become a citizen of this great nation. But I am afraid to say I don't want to be a citizen of the Promised Land." I stammered and stopped as the king raised his thick black eyebrows in surprise and disappointment. I stammered again and continued, "Your Majesty, I stood inside that courtroom for myself and for what I believe in. I believe in love, equal rights, justice and freedom. Those are the values I have been deprived of. Since the day I was born, I was denied these things by my own country and later deprived by my uncle. That is how they all began, the mysteries I've been through during the early years of my life. I am truly honoured today as it is a fact there are thousands of illegal aliens just like me out there who would be delighted to be offered the opportunity of citizenship. But I have been through a lot as a young man and I still have concerns about the thousands of the so-called illegal aliens out there in the Dune who have been thrown out of the walls of the Promised Land and are left to wander the streets. What about their children, who your administration have rejected and want to forcefully send back to the same lion cages from which their fathers and mothers had escaped to bring them to a safe haven? What about the poor and homeless? Your Majesty, I am truly honoured but I must decline your generous offer." I bowed my head and when I raised it again I was eye to eye with the king. His expression was tense, but I held on to my confidence. It seemed as if the sleeping giant within me had finally awakened. I didn't mean to be disrespectful to the king, and I realised even as I was speaking that some people would think it was brave or even foolish of me, a common survivor, to stretch my little claws in front of the biggest cat in the jungle.

But I felt the courage to speak my mind at the dinner table and in the presence of the king, who had the power and authority to throw me out of the royal palace within a blink of an eye. He could just snap his fingers and it would be done.

When I finished addressing the royals, I turned my head to make eye contact with Elena who was already in tears.

"You sound like a brave hunter, Eba," the king said.

"Keep up that spirit young man, for your name will stick on the lips of everyone wherever you decide to spend the rest of your life. But one thing, Eba, don't be a fool like the hunter who let a deer go in order to shoot a bear. I have heard the words that came right from the depth of your heart and through your mouth and I will consider your words carefully, as they highlight some problems on the streets which I have not been aware of. I would suggest you take a little time to consider and reflect on my proposal before making a final decision on it, so I will give you a month to do so. Should you reconsider and decide to take my offer, it will be right here waiting for you. Greetings and have a good evening, enjoy the rest of the tour around the palace." The king left us at the table, his robe dragging on the floor as he retired to his resting chamber.

The queen and the princesses took us around the palace for a tour. We passed through the springing fountain which was electrified with colourful fluorescent lamps fixed on the heads of three golden dragons who spat out water from their mouths in the recycling process. We walked through the fascinating gardens and then to the mini zoo where I saw a caged lion which amazed me the most. I hadn't seen a lion since I left home. The queen was kind to us and spoke to us inspiringly about following our hearts and dreams as it is never too late for dreams to be realised. It was dark by the time we left the palace. We were taken home in a different car driven by a new driver who told us about himself during the ride. His name was Sambo Msambo and he said he had spent all his life serving the royal family. His first job in their employment had been as a servant when he was only twelve years old.

After visiting the palace, I felt like I had bought a halfway ticket for my freedom. I began enquiring about my family back home, and how things were going both politically and socially in my country. I asked Doctor Islaker senior to help me, which she did through an organisation called 'Build It Up Again', an organisation which helped lost people to be reunited with their families.

The organisation soon found out that my uncle, along with some other members of their corrupt political party, had been arrested and sentenced for corruption after their regime was toppled out of power by a people's revolution. 'The New Phase' was a revolutionary group set up by students and supported by the young officers' core of the armed forces. Even though they had taken power illegitimately, they had quickly gained the support of the local people and the international community. Their first priority was to fight corruption and poverty and to make education a human right rather than a privilege. Shortly after taking power, the group proposed to hold a democratic election which they did and then handed back power to civilian rule. I heard from several sources that the organisation 'Build It Up Again' had been operating my homeland, Yougosoba, for the last two years and that they had helped many other people in a similar situation to mine by reuniting them with their families.

Knowing that my uncle and his regime had been toppled gave me confidence. That and the fact that Karamokoh Dambay, the traditional healer, had been brought to justice in front of my own eyes. As for missionary Blaak, I wasn't sure what happened to him, but I hoped he would be cursed and sentenced to search for the holy grail in the depths of the pyramids for eternity, as I later learn he was a part of the conspiracy.

After I learned of the changes in my homeland, I decided to return back home and start a new life. I intended to share my experience with other young people who might be blindly fooled by the myth or fairy tale of the Hundred Golden Horses and the Promised Land.

Having made my decision, I wrote the king a letter in which I reconfirmed the answer I had given him at his dining table, and told him that I had chosen to turn down his offer and return back to my home.

Within a short period, the king replied to me saying that he respected and understood the decision I had reached and suggesting that he might visit me one day in my homeland for a cup of tea and to also learn more about my people.

I had in mind when I return home to sensitise young people by sharing my story so they would think twice before accepting an offer from a stranger who promises to send them away to some fantastical place where they could have a better life.

In this life, people are able to travel and follow their own dreams and they want to explore the world as a human right. But travellers need to be well-informed about the places they go to. In many cases, a helper could become the merchandiser who would exchange them for gold or other favours beyond your imagination.

My Motherland

I couldn't believe it when Elena told me she had made up her mind to follow me back to my homeland. Even though I believed her love for me wasn't a lie, her decision still sounded like a dream to me, a dream which earlier I thought might never come true.

"I will follow you to the end of the world just as I've promised you, Eba," she said.

Sometimes the words that came out of Elena's holy mouth gave me goose pimples on my skin. Elena meant the whole world to me.

I was lucky to return home as a little hero. But there were thousands of my fellow countrymen who were still suffering and many who had perished during their journey to the Promised Land. Even those who did make it had to start all over again, a new struggle with tough challenges. Sometimes people have to start over again and again after several falls. They struggle to survive with the rules, rules that can be the complete opposite to those in their own cultures and traditions.

Those who couldn't stand it would end up being wasted on the streets of the places they had dreamed of. The worst of it was that those wasted lives would never be seen for what they truly are, but for what others think they are.

Elena and I were sitting in the backyard of my father's house, though most of it was shaded by various kinds of trees planted by my ancestors, enjoying the soft tropical evening breeze. When the wind blew the leaves of the mango trees, the sing-song sound they made reminded me of my father.

It had been twelve years since I left this place. I had still been a little boy with a mind occupied by so many dreams, especially dreams of going to school and acquiring an education before returning back to our village to help my father and serve in my community. In all the years since I'd left I hadn't had any contact with my father, but I had always hoped that I would see him alive one day.

There I was, together with the love of my life, on the land on which my father used to pour water on the vegetables and work hard to get rid of the destructive crop pests. Elena and I were there doing nothing but weeping and mourning over the death of the man whose blood runs through my veins. The man I used to call Papa was there no more. From where Elena and I sat, I reflected back to images of me and my father during my childhood, images which made me weep harder. Many of our neighbours came and joined me weeping.

When we had arrived at our village, one of my father's friends explained to us how my father died.

"Your father began suffering from malaria," he told us, "and then after a few years it became worse and turned into some kind of a sickness people here called river blindness. Your father gradually became blind and seriously ill, he suffered all his life until the day he passed away. I could tell he missed you when you were gone."

The man looked up to the sky, bit his lip and said, "I be-lieve that your father is right there in the heavens. He was a good man."

Had there been an empty bucket to collect our tears, I believe that Elena and I could have filled it to the brim as we sobbed during the explanation of my father's friend. At that moment I could see a picture of my father in my head. I could see him asking someone to give him a cup of wa-ter, while he lay on his sickbed. I saw him holding the walls of the dark hallway inside our house to steady himself as he made his way outside to the latrine. I saw him sleeping alone with a hungry belly under a leaking roof during the raining season, drops of rainwater making small holes on the unpaved floor of his bedroom. The images agonised me and I started thinking about taking revenge on my uncle if I ever set my eyes on him again, just like I had done with Samir and his allies.

I found myself thinking about my uncle often, though I re-alised that I couldn't put the blame on someone else for the suffering and death of my father. I thought if my uncle had left me alone when I was a boy, I could have still been there to look after my father when he needed me. When I thought about the pain my father and I had gone through, I felt the veins inside my throat soiling up with guilt, pain and anger.

"It's ok, Eba," Elena cuddled me and reassured me with her soothing voice, that voice of hers which always brings me comfort and calms me. A way of talking to me which Elena was well aware of and had used on many occasions to bring me back to my true self.

Many things had changed in the twelve years I had been

away from my village. I noticed the boss at the carpentry workshop, who used to lash his apprentices on their butts with the wood saw, wasn't there any longer. The apprentices there now seemed to have more comfort and freedom as they learned the trade. They even sat together with their boss to eat their lunch, something that never happened there when I was little. The old boss had always been angry with his apprentices and I frequently witnessed him lashing them. He would tell them to lay on the workbench and beat them severely on their bottoms for the silly mistakes they had made. The son of the old blacksmith, who was one of my friends, had taken over the business after the death of his father. By the time I returned, he was making what he described as modern working tools. The muezzin I used to know when I was little had passed away and been replaced by another one. A new mosque had been built, this time with cement bricks, and painted yellow on most of the top and brown on the bottom which made it look modern. It was within a few days of my return that I realised there was a new muezzin there, when I noticed his voice was far less melodious than the old one.

One morning, as Elena and I were lying on our new wooden bed with a foam mattress, made by the village carpenter, we were awoken by the muezzin's voice in the early morning call. We listened attentively as he began to say the azan, calling people for their prayers. The melody of his voice and the verses he recited took me back to my childhood days, when I was still a boy and would get up early to wake my clan members up for our traditional mango picking. I would spring out of my straw mattress as soon as the cock made its first crow, which would soon be followed by the muezzin's call and the clonking of aluminium pot covers as women from well-to-do families prepared breakfast for their men.

My two early boyhood friends, who I referred to as my partners in crime as we cracked old jokes about those days, were both in their early married lives. Jalil had three children, and Sembu had one child. In that respect, I felt left behind. According to Elena's tradition we were still very young to get married, never mind to have children, while in my tradition a young adult man must find a woman and get married as quickly as possible, before being forced to do so.

"You have a beautiful and exotic woman in your hands. What are you waiting for, Eba?" Sembu had asked me one evening as we took a walk through the woods.

"Well," I said, "Elena and I do love each other to the core, but we are not yet well prepared for it."

"Come on bro," he said, "you are not a boy any longer. I think you have got carried away with the ways of the people in the Promised Land."

"It might be so," I replied. We looked at each other and started to giggle and then dissolved into laughter. I could hear the loud and clear echo of our laughter repeating itself through the thick forest. It was exactly like the way it used to be, the good old days of our boyhood. It had been years since I had laughed like that and I felt wild and free. Boys will always be boys.

Elena was already integrating. She learned how to cook our staple foods and joined other women with daily activities like washing our dirty clothes in the river with their bare hands and singing at night under the shining moonlight.

She also helped people with health problems by setting up a small clinic in our village, operating illegally. Even though according to the law she was living illegally with me, in my village no one is made to feel illegal.

"Your people are very welcoming," Elena told me one afternoon while we were cooking together, "I wish I could have been born here."

"Yes, my people are welcoming to strangers, but please don't wish to have been born here during the time I was born. Life by nature is beautiful here, but it's tough in terms of survival."

"I understand what you mean, Eba, and I have observed a lot since we arrived here. But life is not all about the things we see and want to become. When I look at life here, I see hope in the people and they live in such a natural way. Life is tough for them but they are still smiling and living it their own way."

Elena was full of sympathy for the people she helped, especially for mothers and their malnourished babies. Some of them had to bend over all day, under the hot and burning sun, carrying their dying babies on their back while they searched for ways to save the lives of their young ones. Elena did everything that she could to help the few she was able to, but it wasn't enough. She was the only one around. I could see how Elena wanted to divide herself into two or more to do the job. She often told me that her life sentence was to help people with what she had, especially those in need.

According to my tradition, a man who stays for too long in a relationship out of marriage, not daring to ask for the hand of his girlfriend, is just like a man who has to cross the river to harvest his crop on the other side. Instead of jumping at once into the river and swimming straight to the other side, he keeps walking along the edge of the river looking for a shallow area where he could cross without involving his entire body in swimming.

Sometimes you don't even know where the river ends, or whether you would find a shallow place to cross. It might take you a very long time to figure it out, and your crop could be harvested for you by a stranger who you will never see. Your crop will lose quality while it waits for you, its rightful owner, to quickly cross over the river and harvest it. In the worst case your crop could even be harvested by the farm watch, in order to save a little for you.

People often say that if you want something in this life you have to go out there and get it. That sounds inspiring but when a woman loves a man and wishes to marry him, she will rarely ask the man for it directly.

Elena's genuine intention of spending the rest of her life with me was visible. I could see that in everything she had done in the last three years. I could see her thirst for a lasting matrimonial life since she had returned with me to my home. I could see her love and that, no matter what would happen, she was here and ready to stay.

A year after our return, I had still heard nothing of my uncle or his family and I didn't make any attempt to go and search for them. I had decided that it wasn't worth trying to connect with them. I did consider looking for my cousin, Gina, who used to be the kindest one to me and even taught me to read and write at home. But as for my other cousins,

Sol and Mo, I didn't worry about or miss them much. I occasionally wondered about their mother Agnes and whether she was still tough and mean, and still speaking as loudly as she used to. The issue of extended family is an important value within the norms of my culture and tradition.

When I returned back home, I wasn't the same man I used to be. I was like a new-born man who had been reincarnated in a new culture.

When Elena told me she was one month pregnant, my mouth dropped open in wonder and the announcement that she was carrying the firstborn of our future generation rendered me speechless. She smiled at my astonished expression.

"Are you not happy about becoming a father?"

"Sure, I... am" I stammered uncertainly, though I was excited in my heart.

I had been about to ask Elena to marry me right there and then when she had announced the pregnancy.

We were at the river bank where Elena and I often went for walks, to look at birds and the amazing sunsets. That evening I had asked Elena to go with me to the river, a request which she had refused at first because she was feeling tired. I insisted that she should come with me, and she finally agreed.

I had invited her to the river purposely that evening to propose to her, but it was complicated by the news of her pregnancy and I was uncertain what I should do. I didn't know whether I should proceed with the proposal, or postpone it for another time. A thought whispered in my head, giving me the answer, telling me I should just ask her to marry me right there and then.

I went down to the floor on one knee, dipped my right hand into the front pocket of my shirt and took out a ring which I had made from softwood and asked Elena if she would marry me. She looked at me with quivering lips and at first it looked like she didn't know what to say. She was clearly in shock.

"Yes, Eba, I will marry you."

That moment of happiness was what my people would have described as a double blessing.

Elena's pregnancy announcement reminded me of my mother's story and how she had suffered from miscarriages five times before I was born. That story concerned me as I began to compare my mother's past with Elena's present. But I knew it wasn't logical for me to compare someone's past events to another's present. Besides, Elena was a different person. I thought perhaps it was natural that all men would think like that from the moment their wives announced a pregnancy, and later I loosened up and let go of those thoughts. I smiled at Elena, holding her tight with both my hands wrapped around her body. "Everything is going to be all right," I said.

I felt the warmth of her tears on my shoulder and her chin trembling as she leaned into me. On the other side of the river where it is said I was found after my mother disappeared during the rebel attack in which she died, I held Elena in my arms tightly while she cried. I looked at the spot where it was said I was found crying when I was just a baby and pictured my mother trying to hide me in the tall grass while armed men chased her. One of them pulled the trigger but she continued running to divert their attention away from me and the chase continued to the edge of the river bank where my mother, bleeding from her bullet wounds, threw herself into the water. In the image I saw myself watching my mother's body, a loving farm watch who wanted nothing more than to love and raise her only son, as it floated on the water and drifted downstream on the high tides of the Alligator River.

My imaginations about how my mother was killed were vivid and powerful and they never left me alone, especially when I went to the river.

I wished my mother and father could have been there. I longed for their physical presence, especially at the moment before the main ceremony began.

Overcome with emotions, I went to the garden in our backyard corner and wept in memory of my parents, just like my father had done when his mother passed away.

Elena's parents weren't there either. We had a typical traditional wedding according to my tradition with Elena's consent. Her parents were represented by an elderly couple who were probably around the same age as her mother and father. My parents were represented by my aunt and her husband from my mother's side.

We listened attentively to diverse speeches offering advice about married life by experienced tribal leaders. At the end of the ceremony our right hands were tied together with a white handkerchief as we exchanged our vows in front of the village chief and other traditional leaders.

After we had exchanged our vows of marriage we were officially pronounced husband and wife. The only downside of the ceremony was that I was not allowed to kiss my bride, as to do so in public or in front of the elders is against the morals of our tradition. Elena couldn't stop smiling throughout the exchanging of the rings ceremony. She shed tears of joy, and looked so innocent as those tears streamed down her newly-wedded face while she stared at her official wedding ring. I gave her a golden ring as her bridal prize. A prize for the woman who was about to become the mother of my first-born child.

After the official ceremony we enjoyed a lavish traditional feast. It was not an expensive one, and would have cost us more money if our wedding had taken place in Elena's country. We arranged local drummers from the Djembe group in combination with the Bubu music gang. The musicians played all evening, singing our traditional songs. There were also poets called the Jalibas, who sang songs with words of praise for the newly wedded couple.

There was an abundance of food and, of course, there was plenty of palm wine, freshly tapped from God to man. Otherwise my father the palm wine tapper wouldn't be happy where his remains had been laid to rest. The abundance of everything we needed was because we had just sold some of the crops from our first harvest.

Three years after our return to my motherland, we went to my father's grave to show our respect on the commemoration of his death. The cemetery was in the nearest bushes at the outskirts of our village. My daughter, who we named Bomporo Marion Yoko combining both our mother's names, was also present to grace the occasion. Our sweet and beautiful young princess had already begun to speak our local language, although her mother was working hard to encourage her to learn her own language as well. It was beautiful to mark this important occasion with my wife and child.

After the ritual of palm wine pouring on the grave, I began to speak to my father's spirit. I talked about the things that bothered me most about his death and my struggles, and I introduced my wife and daughter to him.

"Father," I began, "I felt guilty about not being there for you at the time you needed me most. But I do believe you understand."

In those years after I was taken by my uncle, I had to run away and found myself in difficult situations searching for a treasure with no idea where I was going or what the outcome would be. Here I am today presenting to you my daughter, your granddaughter, and my wife, your daughter-in-law. Father, I know you are not coming to us any longer but I believe you are sitting right there in that beautiful river, together with my mother and Elena's father. You are all there waiting for us to join you some day when we leave this world. Father, sleep well and rest in peace. See you in the next life."